NATIVE SON

ELIZABETH C. PHILLIPS
PROFESSOR OF ENGLISH
MEMPHIS STATE UNIVERSITY

MONARCH PRESS

Published with permission of Harper & Row, Publishers, Inc.

Copyright © 1972 by
SIMON & SCHUSTER

All rights reserved. No part of this book may be reproduced in any form without permission in writing from the publisher.

Published by
MONARCH PRESS
a Simon & Schuster division of
Gulf & Western Corporation
Simon & Schuster Building
1230 Avenue of the Americas
New York, N.Y. 10020

Standard Book Number: 0-671-00912-5

Printed in the United States of America

TABLE OF CONTENTS

INTRODUCTION
- Life 1
- Themes 18
- Technique 22

NATIVE SON
- Themes 26
- Techniques 26
- Structure 27
- Book One: Fear 29
- Book Two: Flight 32
- Book Three: Fate 35

CHARACTER ANALYSIS 38

THEMES 65

STYLISTIC QUALITIES
- Contrasts in Symbolic Imagery 74
- Variation in Prose 79

SURVEY OF CRITICISM OF *NATIVE SON*
- The Author's Own 83
- Reviews and Critical Studies 84
- Baldwin and Ellison 86
- Thematic and Formalistic Analyses 88

ESSAY QUESTIONS AND ANSWERS 91

BIBLIOGRAPHY 97

INTRODUCTION: LIFE, THEMES, TECHNIQUE

"A ROOTLESS MAN." There is considerable irony in the fact that an inexpensive copy of Richard Wright's *Eight Men* now reposes in a restricted collection — restricted, that is, for research and against general circulation — of a university library in Memphis, Tennessee. It was in that city, as Mr. Wright himself records in both his essay "The Ethics of Living Jim Crow" and his autobiography *Black Boy*, that he secured books to read only by using a library card borrowed from a Roman Catholic fellow employee and by writing a note requesting the librarian to let "this nigger boy" take out certain books and signing his friend's name.

Such experience, which Mr. Wright differentiates from his earlier Jim Crow education as subtle rather than brutal cruelty, was only one part of a life pattern upon which this Negro author was later to fit his compelling characterization of Bigger Thomas in the novel with which we shall be concerned. From infancy until his removal to Paris after the establishment of his literary reputation, and even beyond that time, Richard Wright felt himself "a rootless man."

CHILDHOOD IN THE SOUTH. He was born on a farm near Natchez, Mississippi in 1908, and taken while quite young to Memphis, where the family, consisting of his parents, himself and a younger brother, lived in a one-story brick tenement. The father's desertion was followed by a period of destitution during which the six-year-old Richard frequented saloons where he was plied with whisky by the amused patrons and where he picked up a vocabulary of obscenities of whose meaning he was completely ignorant. As a consequence, his despairing mother placed his brother and him in an orphan's home. Richard's unhappiness in this crowded, understaffed institution, with its meager food and its hungry, hostile children was so intense that he finally ran away.

The child was then entrusted to the care of various relatives, but he was little happier with members of his family than he had been in an impersonal institution. What he found most intolerable were the efforts of his grandmother, his aunt, and eventually his mother to force him into their own religious practices. Although he gave, under stress, tacit assent to his mother's tearful concern for his soul and allowed himself to be baptized into the Methodist church, he remained intellectually uncommitted.

Alienated by virtue of his intellect and his sensitivity from the black community with which he tried to relate, he found his association with whites even more bewildering. As a very small child, he had puzzled over his grandmother's white skin, but had found his eager questions fended by his mother and had learned to accept the older woman's identification with the Negro culture because of her having a minuscule amount of "Negro blood" in her veins. But it was only when he began to secure jobs with whites in order to supplement the meager family income that he comprehended the breadth of separation between the two societies. White employers' treatment of the small black boy, whom they paid a dollar or so a week for menial chores, ranged from that of the woman who resented his rejection of fermenting molasses and moldy bread to that of a careless ménage, where young Richard was never able to determine exactly what marital, or extra-marital, ties bound various males and females, but where he could eat all the eggs and drink all the milk his starved system craved. Whatever his dietary condition, however, his social degradation remained constant; to his insensitive "superiors" he was something less than human, a being created to do their work and, in their lighter moments, to afford them amusement. Controlling his outrage as far as possible, he submitted to indignities in order to buy clothes and schoolbooks and an occasional sandwich.

EARLY READING. Meanwhile, his voracious appetite for reading was being partially satisfied by the magazine supplement of a newspaper he sold at the suggestion of a school friend. A serialization of *Riders of the Purple Sage* by Zane Grey, the writer whose tales of the American West were so popular in the early decades of this century; cheap versions of what is now called science-fiction; badly written and highly improbable adventure stories — all excited his eager mind and made him aware of a world which, with his limited background, he had not dreamed existed. But this source of vicarious fulfillment was cut short when a family friend, a carpenter at whose home he called to sell a paper, pointed out that the news section, which young Richard had never read, was devoted to vicious anti-Negro, Ku Klux Klan propaganda. Ashamed and terrified that the black community might feel that he was in league with its most dreaded enemy, he threw his remaining papers away. But he continued to read avidly, spending such time as was not taken up by his studying at the Jim Hill public school in Jackson devouring tattered, second-hand copies of such pulp magazines as Flynn's *Detective Weekly* or *Argosy*.

FIRST PUBLICATION. These formative years of Richard's life were shadowed by his mother's recurrent illness. During one of their stays in Arkansas, she had suffered a paralytic stroke, and although there were brief periods of partial recovery, she never completely regained her health. Her son's love and his sense of responsibility furnished additional distraction, and yet he managed not only to continue at school but to achieve his first publication. A story imaginatively titled *The Voodoo of Hell's Half-Acre* was printed, with no pay for its author, in a local Negro newspaper. But this aspiring young writer missed the praise and encouragement usually accompanying such achievement: his relatives considered the story sinful; his schoolmates, a foolish waste of time; and even the school principal, who might have been expected to exhibit pride in an exceptionally gifted student, disapproved of the use of the word *hell* in the title!

VALEDICTORIAN. That same principal attempted, when Richard was made valedictorian of his graduating class — it was only the ninth grade instead of the twelfth possible for young persons in other regions and of another color — to write his speech for him, a neatly turned out address which consisted of high-sounding banalities calculated not to offend the sensibilities of whites who might be counted on to recommend this bright colored boy for a scholarship to some Negro college. To the bewilderment of both the principal and an uncle of Richard's who had taught school, the young man refused, and on graduation night delivered a speech written by himself.

Thus in 1925 at the age of seventeen, Richard Wright faced the world with nine years of formal education, all he was ever to have. His immediate problem was identical with that of past years, finding work to support himself and to supplement the meager family income. He tried various jobs. First he was porter in a store that sold inferior products to Negroes at marked-up prices and on credit that insured perpetual debt for the purchaser; then there was work in an optical company where his hopes of learning a trade were dashed by envious white fellow-employees; next there was employment in a drug-store where his determined effort to assume an inferiority he did not feel resulted in a nervous fatigue that impeded his movements and led eventually to his dismissal. And finally he worked in a hotel, first as a hallboy, powerless to demonstrate the hot resentment he felt at the insulting familiarities taken by the white night-watchman with the Negro maids, and then as a bellboy, one of whose duties was providing bootleg liquor for the white prostitutes whose nakedness when the contraband was delivered to their rooms was supposed to be completely ignored by the young black man they regarded as less than human.

CRIME AS TRANSITION. The time came when Richard knew he could no longer endure this existence; that he could never adapt, as others of his race were doing, to a culture that demanded of him a constant role-playing of a grinning, obeisant clown; and that if he attempted any longer to force himself into dissimulation totally foreign to his nature there would be a violent eruption and he would kill or be killed, perhaps both. Having no legal means of securing enough money for railroad fare and for sustaining him until additional work could be secured — he had hit on one hundred dollars as the amount he would need — he resolved to steal. The decision was agonizing and so, quite literally, was the procedure. It involved holding out a number of tickets during the rush hour at the Negro movie house where he accepted a night job at the suggestion of another hotel worker who casually informed him that having served a six-months jail sentence precluded his own involvement. As a result of his collusion with the box-office girl who resold the tickets brought to her from the sweating Richard by still another accomplice, he possessed, after a grueling week's ill-gotten gains had been divided, a total of fifty dollars. Fearing further risk of arrest and the chain gang, the dreaded penal labor imposed on the Southern lawbreaker, particularly if he were black, Richard resolved to secure the remainder of the required sum by a further incursion into crime. He stole a gun from a neighbor and pawned it under an assumed name; and with the aid of two adventurous acquaintances, he broke into the storeroom of a Negro college and carried off cans of preserved fruits to sell in restaurants.

Thus provided with enough money to take him to Memphis and tide him over until work could be secured, he slipped out of the Jackson home without the knowledge of any of his relatives except his mother. Bidding her good-bye, he evaded her anxious questions as to whether he had done anything wrong, and promised to send for her as soon as possible.

OUTSIDE THE LAW. When he finally boarded the Jim Crow coach, the only section of the train where a Negro was permitted to ride, he discovered that out of his cumulative anxiety and his present partial release from the fears of the past weeks, he was weeping. And he realized, he says, the suffering that crime effects in the wrongdoer himself. He fervently hoped that he would never again be forced into crime. His hope was realized. Although the success and fame of his later years were still far in the future, the Jackson episode was his only venture into illegality. That he writes of it with unflinching honesty is a demonstration of his integrity. But the account of his thievery is more than that; it is an indictment of a society which forced a person of his capabilities into such shameful behavior as the only means of escaping its shackles and of fulfilling those capabilities. And although he makes abundantly clear that his crime was never repeated, he does not thereby dissociate himself from less fortunate members of his race. He mentions the cooks who habitually stole from their employers' kitchens enough food to compensate partially for the meager wages they received and to feed families who would have starved if they had been dependent on those wages. He further mentions a neighbor who stole bags of grain from a wholesale house where he worked and the bellboys who took whatever they could at the hotel. Again, he relates this condition to the total structure of black and white relationship, in which the white man, creator and guardian of the laws governing society, decrees that the Negro is outside the laws, so far as any protection is concerned, but nonetheless demands that he obey them. Understanding this clearly, Richard was able to convince himself that being outside the laws, as the white man had told him by word and deed, he was not bound to obey them. As we shall see, this ability to identify with blacks whose moral natures, unlike his own, were hopelessly distorted and stunted by a system from which they could never escape, found expression in his fiction and pre-eminently in his creation of Bigger Thomas.

ARRIVAL IN MEMPHIS. But the writing of *Native Son* was still far in the future when young Richard arrived in Memphis. Though he had lived there as a small child, the intervening years had been spent in smaller places, and so on that cold November morning in 1925 he exhibited something of the country boy's wariness of the big city, determined not to be taken in by metropolitan wiles nor to expose his own lack of sophistication. His extreme caution led to an amusing error. Finding his way to Memphis's famous Beale Street, he recalled the stories he had heard of its wickedness and its dangers, of the pickpockets and cutthroats who menaced property and life, and of the prostitutes and confidence men who pursued their victims with less violence but no less rapacity. His first concern was securing a place to live; carrying his suitase, he walked several blocks on Beale until he came to a frame house with a *Rooms* sign in the window. He still hesitated, however, for he could not be certain whether this was a bona fide rooming house or a house of prostitution. His worst fears were confirmed when, having summoned enough courage to walk up the steps, he saw a big mulatto woman staring out the window. When she smiled at him, he turned to leave, certain that he had been about to enter one of the brothels for which the street was notorious. It was not until her insistent call summoned the reluctant young man back and he uneasily answered her probing questions that he discovered the authenticity of her *Rooms* sign and the respectability of her home. Her perspicacity at his mistake and the easy humor with which she accepted it soon put him at ease, and he gratefully rented the proffered room, where, relaxed and heartened by this unexpected encounter with simple kindliness, he fell into restful sleep.

But his stay with his landlady, Mrs. Moss, was not to be the tranquil interlude he had hoped for. Although the motherly woman continued to display a gratifying trust in the character of the young refugee from Mississippi, that trust assumed disturbing new dimensions when it became evident that she had immediately chosen him as a husband for her nubile seventeen-year-old daughter Bess. Nothing in Richard's previous experience had prepared him for the directness with which both mother and daughter set about adding him to the household. Touched by their ready acceptance of his humanity, which others, both black and white, had rejected, he was nonetheless aware of the threat to his life's plan and escaped as soon as decency and gratitude permitted.

NUANCES IN CRUELTY. We noted earlier that Mr. Wright discussed his experiences with white society during this second period in Memphis in a provocative essay entitled "The Ethics of Living Jim Crow." Although, as he states, the cruelty he encountered now was subtler than the physical brutality directed toward him earlier, it was not free from violence. One of the most horrifying portions of *Black Boy*, the autobiographical work covering his first nineteen years, is the account of his being paid by white employers for a boxing match with another Negro boy, after unsuccessful attempts on the part of the former to persuade each that the other was planning to kill him.

The fight was a brutal display of sadism on the part of the white men who crowded into a basement on Main Street. Neither women nor Negroes, other than the two boys, were admitted. The obscenities shouted at the fighters intensified Richard's feeling of shame and degradation, already nearly intolerable because of his self-disgust at allowing himself to be duped into inflicting and enduring pain. He managed to avoid subsequent fights, but whenever he heard of other young Negroes being exploited in similar fashion, his sense of having committed a foul and unforgivable sin recurred.

Young Richard's first employment in Memphis was as a dishwasher in a Main Street café, but it soon occurred to him that his past experience in an optical company in Jackson might now stand him in good stead. Carefully refraining from expressing any hope of advancement and frankly admitting in his interview with a manager of a Memphis optical concern that he had been run off his Jackson job by a white boy who resented his ambition, he was employed at eight dollars a week. His work consisted largely of running errands, washing eye-glasses as they came from the machines, and carrying packages to the post office. A supplement to his income came from performing every conceivable service for white workers during his lunch hour, the tips he received making it possible for him to save a considerable sum. Meantime he was gradually learning to conceal the tension he felt around whites.

DISCOVERY OF H. L. MENCKEN. Reference has been made

earlier to his securing books through a ruse. The authors to whose work he was thus introduced were to have a profound effect upon his thinking and his own writing. As is invariably the case with a careful reader possessed of lively intellectual curiosity, one reading experience led him directly to another of even greater excitement. For example, his first acquaintance with the writing of H. L. Mencken, the famous iconoclast who gleefully hurled his wit-laden missiles at many a cherished American delusion in the nineteen-twenties and thirties, came through an editorial in the Memphis *Commercial Appeal*. Through the kindly offices of a Negro porter in a bank, Richard could read the paper before he went to work and thus save five cents for his lunch. One day he read an angry attack on Mencken. Knowing at this time only that Mencken was editor of a magazine, the *American Mercury*, the young man wondered what a magazine editor could have done to incur the wrath of a local editor. He shrewdly surmised that Mr. Mencken must have been propounding ideas distasteful to the South. And this led him to a startling supposition: there must be others besides Negroes who dared to criticize the South. Furthermore, he felt a kind of affinity for a writer, who, like himself, aroused hatred. Consequently, on his next visit to the library he presented a forged note requesting some books by H. L. Mencken.

After this encounter with a writer who had the courage to attack and criticize, and whose style was different from any young Richard had met before, he went on to the authors whose names so freely scattered about Mencken's lively pages elicited his interest. Among them were Edgar Allan Poe, O. Henry, and Mark Twain, known to generations of American schoolboys more fortunately situated than Richard, a boy who had experienced a thrill of satisfaction at Zane Grey's superficial fictionizing of the American west but had been deprived of the pleasurable terror of Poe's stories and the rollicking humor of the other two writers. But of those mentioned by Mencken, Theodore Dreiser, the great American naturalistic novelist, and Sinclair Lewis, the Dickensian satirist of American types, proved particularly influential. Dreiser's *An American Tragedy* dealt with many of the deleterious economic and social trends in our country which Wright was to focalize in Black experience in *Native Son*. Lewis' *Main Street* led Richard to see that a small town can have stultifying effects even on privileged white inhabitants, and *Babbitt,* with its depiction of the American businessman who cannot escape from the conformist atmosphere stifling his individuality, gave the young Negro a better understanding of his white "bosses" who suffered in their own turn from crippling frustration.

PLANS FOR MOVING NORTH. With a secure if unsatisfying job, Richard was able to carry out his plan for bringing his mother and brother to Memphis. In the household thus established, he had warm meals at regular hours and discovered, to his surprise, that he could read faster. But even though his situation was improved, life in the South offered no hope of personal fulfillment. So once again plans were made for moving North. When his brother also secured a job, the two began saving money and tried setting dates for departure. Meanwhile, Richard was very careful to tell none of the white men with whom he worked that he was leaving the South, for he knew it would alter their attitude toward him. He felt that there would be an intuitive realization on their part, whether consciously formulated or not, that his leaving meant he was not happy with them. Thus, the image they cherished of the carefree "darky," content to live one day at a time and grateful for any favors gratuitously bestowed by white superiors would have to be revised, and their self-image might be threatened.

But however carefully he guarded his intentions, he had already clearly assessed what his life in the South would be. The variety of possibilities offered no satisfactory choice for him. Banding with other Negroes in opposition to Southern whites would be futile because Negroes were outnumbered and lacked strength. Submitting to the system and accepting the status of amiable slavery was repugnant to his very nature. Nor would marrying the willing Bess and inheriting her mother's property afford much greater liberty. The transferal of hatred of self to others with black skins, and the resultant brawling with other Negroes would require a coldness of which he was incapable. Escape from his frustrations through a series of casual intimacies with available women and through habitual drunkenness was too near the course his father had taken and would, in addition, be as much a violation of his inmost being as those indignities inflicted on him by others. Finally, that avenue by which a few Southern Negroes escaped hardship and degradation, entrance into a profession such as law or medicine or teaching, was closed to him. Not only had he lacked opportunity for training, he had almost no acquaintance with prosperous, successful Negroes, and he found their world almost as foreign as the white world. His awareness of his complete inability to make any kind of adjustment to Southern living kept him in a state of almost unbearable tension, compounded by a very real dread that, in spite of all his efforts at self-control and the dissembling of his actual feelings, he would some day break loose and commit an act that would destroy his life before any of the fruition for which he longed could come about.

The event which precipitated the actual move to Chicago was the visit of his aunt, whose husband had deserted her and who was now trying to find means of supporting herself. As the four persons, his mother, his aunt, his brother, and himself, held their anxious consultations as to the feasible ways of carrying out their plans, it became apparent that they could not wait until they were fully prepared. They would never have enough money, and so there would always be the risk of starving. That being the case, one time was as good as another. Consequently, the desperate decision was made. Richard and his aunt would go first, and immediately, and then send for the other two when they had found jobs and shelter.

FINAL HUMILIATION. However, one gruelling confrontation had to be endured before leaving Memphis. Richard had to tell his white employer he was going North, and had to prevent the opposition such an announcement would inevitably arouse from flaring into open hostility or some kind of forcible restraint. He managed by a very simple expedient, a series of lies concerning his reason for leaving, his attitude toward his present job, and his opinions of life in the North. He told the "boss" that his family was going and he had to go with them; cheerfully acceded to the facetious suggestion that he, a man of nineteen, would have to be very careful not to fall into Lake Michigan; offered fervent protestations of his gratitude for being employed at the optical factory and his pleasure in working there; and humbly promised not to speak to white girls when he reached the North. His deceptive powers were strained to the utmost by his response to the white man's querulous insistence that "niggers" always changed when they went North. Richard glibly asserted that he would never change, successfully repressing his impulse to tell the other that a wish to change was his impelling motive.

The gripping and poignant *Black Boy* concludes with a recapitulation of Richard Wright's feelings as he rode the train to Chicago the next day. He was leaving the South, he recalls, without the slightest twinge of regret, for it had treated him with nothing but hatred and contempt. The only satisfactions he had found were in books, and the result was a vicarious and intangible existence. From those books by H. L. Mencken and Sinclair Lewis, as we have already seen, and others by the poet Edgar Lee Masters and by Sherwood Anderson, author of the Impressionistic stories of a small town, *Winesburg, Ohio*, he gained the idea that America could be shaped into something nearer the ideal on which it was founded. He also felt that, in a way not fully clear, he could be a part of the ideal.

Although the white South had prided itself on its knowledge of "niggers," a class of inferior beings to which he was consigned, it had never had any knowledge of him. Forcing him into a way of life least conducive to the development of high moral and ethical consciousness, it had come close to making him the kind of being it imagined him. He had lied, he had cheated, he had stolen, and it may have been, he says, a mere accident that he had never killed. He had never been fully himself because the South had never permitted him to be. So he was leaving it in order to find himself and to fully understand what the South had done to him and all his people.

If Mr. Wright had stopped there, we might only partially understand his writing. It is only what he says further that enables us to grasp the full import of his literary work, particularly the novel with which we shall be concerned.

WRIGHT'S HOPE, FAULKNER'S HOPE. In another sense, he says, he would never be able actually to depart from the South, for it had molded him, and his very being was permeated with its culture. Thus, even though he left it bodily, he was taking a part of it with him. And he hoped that that part, under different circumstances from any he had yet known, would be transmitted into something beautiful and true. If that should happen, he says, then he would have hope for the South itself, the hope that the South could overcome its violence and its cruelty, and could transcend its guilty heritage. Students who have read the South's most famous white writer, William Faulkner, will recall that he cherished a similar hope. In one of Faulkner's best treatments of Southern guilt, *The Bear*, the white protagonist Isaac McCaslin makes a conscious effort to atone for that guilt. But when, in December 1927, Richard Wright left the South for Chicago, Faulkner's best work was yet to be written. There was no way for the young black dreamer to know that a white Southerner shared his dreams.

At first, life in Chicago was no easier for Richard than it had been in the South. The cold penetrated to his very bones and work was not easy to find. Although no autobiographical account of his life after 1927 is as fully detailed as *Black Boy*, he has recorded many of the events and impressions of those first years in Chicago in the last section of his book *Eight Men*. The story "The Man Who Went to Chicago" tells of his first employment with a kindly Jewish couple who operated a delicatessen, and with whom he never felt at ease because his previous experience with white employers had not prepared him for their acceptance of him as a human being.

From this job he went to that of postal clerk, having passed a Civil Service examination. Since it was a night job, he could use the greater part of his days in eagerly expanding his knowledge by reading and in laboring feverishly at his own writing. Meantime, his mother and brother had joined him, alleviating his loneliness but adding to his responsibilities.

Like all Americans, especially those whose economic situation was precarious at best, Richard suffered from the Depression which followed the stock market crash of 1929. His post office job was no more; the only work he could find was that of an insurance agent for a Negro burial society, a distasteful employment because it involved defrauding ignorant black people to guarantee profit for the owners of the business. His misery at this exploitation and at the squalid poverty which made it possible was only slightly lessened by the casual intimacies he enjoyed, like all the other agents, with black women who could pay their minimal premiums in no other way.

WRITER ON RELIEF. Even that job came to an end, and with his mother's illness and impending starvation, Richard was forced to go on relief. Humiliating as this expedient was, however, it had its bright side, for his case worker was the wife of the University of Chicago sociologist, Dr. Louis Wirth. Through the Wirths, the young man first secured work as a hospital orderly and then in a Boys Club where his understanding of his own people was deepened by daily association with youngsters whose deprivation equaled, or exceeded, that of his own childhood. And an even more direct impetus to his writing career was furnished by a job as publicity writer for the Federal Negro Theatre, itself under the sponsorship of the Works Project Administration. Of equal significance to his development as a literary personage was his position with the Illinois Writers Project.

WRIGHT AS A COMMUNIST. The Chicago years also saw the beginnings of his long association with the Communist party. For the full story of this association, which lasted until 1944, the student should read Mr. Wright's own account, as told in an article entitled "I Tried to Be a Communist, " full bibliographic data for which will be found in the present Study Guide. To fully appreciate, however, his treatment of Communism in *Native Son*, a few details concerning his own experience will be helpful. His first connection came through the John Reed Club, a club founded by the Communists to encourage the development of literary talent which could be utilized for Party purposes, and named for the young American poet and journalist, whose political idealism led him to Moscow, where he died of typhus during the Revolution in 1920 and where his tomb became a shrine.

Richard Wright's participation in the club resulted in the publication of his poems, stories, and essays in *New Masses* and other left-wing journals. He joined the Communist party in 1932 and worked for it both as organizer and writer for many years. Even in the first years, however, and in spite of his belief that the Negro's hope could be realized through this party, he found himself in opposition to its leaders and its rigid, impersonal discipline.

In 1937, he went to New York as Harlem editor of the *Daily Worker*. All this time, he was steadily writing and his work was being published in reputable magazines with no political affiliations, such as *Story*. His literary reputation was sufficiently well established by now for the aspiring young writer Ralph Ellison, who achieved his own fame later through the novel *Invisible Man*, to come to him for guidance.

Always attractive to women, Wright found himself now in circles where racial differences erected no barrier. Two white women whom he first knew in 1938 were Ellen Poplar, who like himself worked as an organizer for the Communists, and Rose Dhima Meadman, who had distinguished herself in modern dance. He and Rose were married in 1939, a year which also brought increasing literary recognition: he was awarded a Guggenheim Fellowship, which enabled him to complete *Native Son*, and a short story, "Bright and Morning Star," was chosen by Edward O'Brien, critic and editor, as one of the two best of the year as well as one of the fifty best since 1915.

"NATIVE SON" APPEARS. Publication of *Native Son* came in 1940. During that year Richard and Rose moved to Cuernavaca, the city in Mexico which has attracted so many artists and writers from all over the world. But he was not happy in the new country and his unhappiness was aggravated by the widening of a rift between his wife and him. He returned alone to the United States, visiting most of the places whose association with his childhood and youth we have noted, in order to relive past experiences as preparation for the writing of his autobiography. Perhaps the most poignant encounter was with his father, who had long since returned to Natchez, Mississippi, where he once again became a sharecropper. As Mr. Wright tells of their meeting, he notes with sadness the gulf that separated them. Although he saw in his father's face features he had himself inherited, and although the fierce resentment he had once felt at the older man's desertion had changed to an aching pity, he could find no way to communicate with the aging, beaten man. They no longer spoke the same language.

Back in New York, Richard began seeing Ellen Poplar once more and on March 12, 1941, they were married. Two other significant happenings were the production in Orson Welles's Mercury Theatre of a stage version of *Native Son*, and the bestowal of the Spingarn Medal by the NAACP, an award given annually to a Negro whose achievements were considered noteworthy.

Richard and Ellen Wright had two children, both daughters. The first, Julia, was born in New York in 1942; the second, Rachel, in Paris in 1949. During those years occurred changes which would be reflected in his subsequent writing. His final break with the Communist party came in 1944, and in 1946 he made his first visit to France, where the liberating effect of his acceptance as a gifted person and the absence of racial discrimination led to his decision to make his home there.

Before he left his native land, however, further literary recognition came to him. His autobiography, *Black Boy*, which, as we have noted, treated his childhood and youth, was published in 1945 and was widely read and acclaimed.

The second of the younger writers to whom his success was inspiration and encouragement paid him a visit. Just as Ralph Ellison had done earlier, James Baldwin, whose fame as the author of *Go Tell It On the Mountain* and of collections of brilliant essays and of other novels was later to equal or even outstrip Wright's own, came to the older man to pay tribute to his greatness and to ask advice as a beginning writer.

EXPATRIATE IN FRANCE. Living in France, Richard Wright found opportunity for greater philosophical and artistic development. His close association with Jean-Paul Sartre and Simone de Beauvoir, famous for their existential philosophy as well as their creative writing, is reflected in novels such as *The Outsider* and *Savage Holiday*. And his increasing discouragement with the power struggle between the Soviet Union and the United States led to a conviction that human rights and international stability would have to come from the Third World, that is, the non-white, non-European countries. Keenly aware of his African heritage, even though, like all American descendants of slaves, he had been sharply cut off from any knowledge of his cultural past, he involved himself with notable Africans, among them the Senegalese writer, Alioune Diop.

A contract with an Argentine film company for a motion picture of *Native Son* necessitated return visits to the United States where exterior shots were made in Chicago. He not only wrote the scenario, but, perhaps ill-advisedly, he played the role of Bigger Thomas. The student will have to decide for himself, after a careful examination of the novel, whether Wright's understanding of this uneducated young black man, so completely at the mercy of both the white world and his own uncontrollable impulses, counteracts the obvious differences in intellect and appearance between the author and his creation. Photographs from the film do not, somehow, quite fit the reader's image of Bigger. Nor was the movie favorably reviewed in the United States, a circumstance Wright felt, perhaps with justification, was due to politically-motivated cutting by American distributors which destroyed its artistic unity. On the other hand, the unedited European version was widely praised by continental reviewers.

During the last ten years of his life, Richard Wright continued the production of major works; none of which, however, exhibits quite the power of *Native Son*. Among these were the two novels previously mentioned, *The Outsider* and *Savage Holiday; Black Power*, which grew out of visits to the Gold Coast of Africa; *The Color Curtain*, an account of the Bandung, Indonesia conference on Asian-African concerns; *Pagan Spain*, resulting from a visit to the country of the title; *White Man, Listen!*, a collection of lectures; and his last novel, *The Long Dream*.

Among great persons who found their way to Wright's home near Ailly in Normandy, where he had bought an old farm as a retreat from the busy life of Paris, was Dr. Martin Luther King, Jr.

As conditions in France became politically unstable, Mr. Wright made plans to move to London, where Julia had gone for study at Cambridge after distinguishing herself at the Sorbonne. But for reasons which have never been satisfactorily explained, the British government refused him a visa, and he returned to Paris, where he died of a heart attack on November 28, 1960. After cremation, his ashes were buried in the Cimitier Du Pere Lachaise in Paris.

WRIGHT'S MAJOR THEMES. Although Richard Wright's expanding knowledge of twentieth-century society, especially through his ever-widening circle of friends after he took up residence in Europe, led him to treat more than one of our century's major issues, his major theme remained the life of the American Negro. Mr. Wright consistently treated that life as it was shaped, or misshaped, by the dominant white culture.

His first major treatment of the theme is found in a collection of short stories entitled *Uncle Tom's Children.* The pieces in this book are concerned with the hardships of Negro sharecroppers in the South. In spite of the fact that no character in the stories is a typical "Uncle Tom," in the sense that he plays the role imposed upon him by circumstances and thus pleases his white persecutors (a curious distortion, incidentally, of the characterization in Harriet Stowe's famous nineteenth-century novel, *Uncle Tom's Cabin,* the protagonist of which practices Christian virtue but refuses to carry out wicked commands), Wright was not satisfied with his work. He felt that it might elicit tears from white readers but no genuine change in attitude; so his aim in his next work was to write of the black man's life in such a way that it would confront the white reader without the consolation weeping might afford. Thus the theme of *Native Son* became the *brutalizing effect of American society upon a young Negro, and that society's refusal to accept the consequences of its own sins.*

Variations on this theme occur in a collection of short stories, *Eight Men.* The volume was first published in 1961, but the separate tales comprising it date from as far back as 1937. In each the protagonist is a black man, and in four of them the protagonist is defeated by forces he cannot circumvent, whether in hopelessly underpaid farm work in the South, as in "The Man Who Was Almost a Man" and "The Man Who Saw the Flood," or in a succession of menial jobs from which the only escape is a crime anticipated and prejudged by the white guardians of the law in some large Northern city, as in "The Man Who Lived Underground" and "The Man Who Killed a Shadow." The other four, however, afford some measure of triumph for the title character. We have already noted that "The Man Who Went to Chicago" deals with Mr. Wright's own experiences which, difficult and rigorous as they were, did not destroy him. Similarly, the chief character in "Big Black Good Man" is a huge sailor whose strength and blackness terrify the Danish porter of a cheap Copenhagen hotel, but who is revealed as amiably generous, his ominous circling of the white man's scrawny neck with his tremendous fingers proving a measuring device for the half dozen expensive shirts he brings later as a gift. "Man of All Work" also displays a comedic turn, its hero recovering from the gunshot wound inflicted by a jealous wife whose husband has made passes at the supposed housemaid who is really an anxious young husband and father disguised in women's clothes. And although there is terror in "Man, God Ain't Like That," its black hero, in this case a native African, escapes unscathed after the ritual murder in Paris of the white employer he reverences as a Christ who will rise again — escapes because the French police regard his confession as the ravings of a religious fanatic. Even in the stories in which the black man avoids destruction, however, the conflict between him and the white world is treated, as is the white man's total failure to understand his motives and to regard him as a fellow human being.

Conflict is still present in the novel written after Mr. Wright's removal to Europe had furthered his acquaintance with such philosophies as those of the nineteenth-century German, Friedrich Nietzsche, and the Danish philosopher, Sören Kierkegaard, as well as the existentialism of his good friend Jean-Paul Sartre. However, in *The Outsider*, the Negro protagonist, Cross Damon, is unlike Bigger Thomas in himself rejecting all American middle-class values. Thus, *the theme of black-white struggle merges into a criticism of Western society itself*. Mr. Wright further presented that criticism in a novel which employs all white characters, *Savage Holiday*.

AFRICAN THEMES. As he learned more about African nationalism, with the emergence of his ancestral land as a power to be reckoned with in the modern world, Richard Wright incorporated his increased knowledge as an additional theme in his work. We saw how one of the stories in *Eight Men* deals with a young African's confused interpretation of Christian doctrine. Africa and its specialized problems are also treated in such nonfiction works as, *Black Power: A Record of Reactions in a Land of Pathos* and *The Color Curtain: A Report on the Bandung Conference*.

Regardless of a conscientious attempt, however, to understand and to interpret for readers the significance of the "Dark Continent," Richard Wright was always, as he discovered, more Western than African. Consequently, in the last novel to be published during his lifetime, *The Long Dream*, he was once more concerned with what, in the last analysis, is his major theme, the struggle of an American Negro born in the South to make a place for himself in the country which gives him birth but denies him his birthright.

MARXIAN MOTIF. There is one remaining theme which should not be overlooked. Every socially conscious individual must adopt some political belief as the fittest expression of his social ideals. Though Richard Wright was eventually to become as disillusioned with Communism as he had been with American capitalism, a disillusionment which led to his renouncing the Party permanently in 1944, there was a period, beginning in 1932, when it seemed to him that it offered the Negro a satisfactory ideology. Thus, much of his writing presents the Party in a favorable light. For a full account of his experience as a party member, the reader should turn to the *Atlantic Monthly* article, published in two issues, August and September, 1944, "I Tried to Be a Communist." But *expressions of the Marxian ideal*, whose brave slogan "From each according to his ability, to each according to his need" has appealed to many a high-minded young person, regardless of color, are to be found in much of his fiction of the 1930's and 40's, including *Native Son*. We shall see in that novel how, although Bigger himself has been conditioned to regard Communism as a vague evil, two of his staunchest supporters are Party members: the young white man who offers him genuine friendship, Jan Erlone; and the brilliant lawyer who puts all his knowledge and eloquence into Bigger's defense, Boris A. Max.

BLACK MAN, WHITE WORLD. In summary, Richard Wright's main themes all relate to the black man in a hostile society. They include the hardships and frustrations endured by the Southern Negro sharecropper, the misery and injustice suffered by the black man in large cities, and the devastation wrought upon personal and societal relationships by the black man's awareness of separation and alienation. Other themes are ideologies which seem to offer hope, particularly Communism; the general inadequacy of Western values; and the increasing significance of Africa in world affairs. And there is still another theme in all of Mr. Wright's work, a theme which transcends pessimism and despair, man's potential for good.

WRIGHT'S TECHNIQUE. Although Richard Wright began to publish somewhat later than major naturalistic American writers such as Theodore Dreiser, it was in the *naturalistic tradition* that he began, that *school of writing which shows man at the mercy of vast impersonal forces, both biological and economic*. In such fiction a neatly developed plot with a recognizable inception, rising action that mounts steadily to a climax, and falling action that leads to a denouement, or winding up of all loose ends, is neither essential nor appropriate. So it is that the structure of both Mr. Wright's novels and shorter fiction often appears out of balance and lacking in proportion.

But what his work lacks in balance it makes up for in *intensity*. Events move swiftly, often in a crescendo of horror. And the emotions of the characters are so realistically presented as to evoke from the reader corresponding feelings. *Suspense* also is created in much of Mr. Wright's fiction; in "The Man Who Lived Underground," for example, the reader hopes against hope that the protagonist will be able to resume life above ground and that he will be able to convey his sense of human interdependence even to the police who first wrung a false confession from him. It is only on the last page that a policeman's bullet ends his life before a manhole cover consigns his body to the whirling waters of the sewer from which he had escaped.

Not only does choice of incident enhance the effectiveness of Richard Wright's work but also the *quality of his prose*. Though his formal education was limited, he read widely and consciously experimented in style. As a consequence, his very sentence patterns convey the intended effect, short and abrupt when action is rapid, longer and more rhythmical when a character's vision or sleeping dream is presented.

Richard Wright is particularly skillful in *dialogue*, whether the speech is that of the educated or the dialect of the unlettered black. For the latter he carefully reproduces, through his own kind of phonetic spelling, such characteristics as elision or the dropping of consonants. For example, "to tell" becomes "t tell," without the apostrophe conventionally used by dialect writers to indicate omission, or "ain't that" becomes "ain tha." To a reader who has heard such speech, the transcription rings true, and even for one who has never heard this dialect, the feeling is somehow right as the very appearance of the unfamiliar spelling on the printed page seems to fit the total picture.

Another outstanding characteristic of Richard Wright's style is his *imagery*. Every kind of sensory image is employed to produce the effect which the author desires. Color abounds, as when Fred Daniels, in "The Man Who Lived Underground" strikes a match in the dark sewer, and it first produces a greenish glow and then turns red and orange and finally yellow; or when, after some light enters from above, he sees a pool of gray-green liquid from which there arises at intervals a large bubble that glistens blue and purple before it bursts.

Auditory images are used with equal skill. In the short story which provides an adumbration of Bigger's crime in *Native Son*, "The Man Who Killed a Shadow," Saul Saunders becomes accustomed to the siren of the police car in the Negro sections of cities, but because it betokens peril, he hears it again in the screams of a neurotic white woman and is forced to kill her in order to silence the scream that means death for him.

Also utilized to produce the effect of organic vitality are images of scent and taste. When Daniels, of "The Man Who Lived Underground," first lets himself into the sewer, his lungs are filled with the stench of rot. In contrast to such an offensive image, however, are gustatory images introduced into the same story. When the chief character has made his way into a basement and then into a fruit store, he assuages his hunger by removing from under their mosquito-netting cover pears, oranges, bananas, peaches and plums, biting into the juicy peaches and pears, and sucking the oranges after making a small hole with his teeth. The sheer sensuous delight of this passage is not unlike that evoked by the poetry of John Keats, the British Romantic whose joy in all the pleasures of the senses afforded compensation even in the face of early death.

Finally, Richard Wright's technique includes the use of forceful and frequently shocking *symbols*. But these symbols are rarely, if ever, wrenched out of context for the sake of impact on the reader. Rather, they are intrinsic elements of whatever area of environment is being presented on the narrative level, and thus their effect is two-fold: the reader experiences them with his senses, as in the case of the imagery with which we have just been concerned, but he is also made aware that they stand for more than their surface appearance. We shall examine this technique in greater detail in our analysis of *Native Son*. For the present, two examples will suffice, drawn like many of the representative images just considered, from the memorable short story, "The Man Who Lived Underground." Both evoke horror and revulsion, and both symbolize the evil of the world above the sewer, evil which the protagonist cannot escape even by going underground. When the frightened man is making his way cautiously through the ominous darkness, almost slipping on the slimy floor, he hears a rustle and feels a live thing brushing by him. Striking a match he sees a large rat, its coat soaked in the nauseous liquid of the sewer. Such a symbol is perhaps even more shocking today than when Mr. Wright's story was first published, since research aimed at the improvement of living conditions for all Americans has revealed that many of the poor still live amid rat-infested squalor. But within this story and, as we shall see later in the novel *Native Son*, the rat becomes the symbol not only of filth and danger, but of a human being forced by a society he did not make into a pattern of skulking dirtiness and aggressive menace. The second symbol surpasses the first in horror. It is the tiny nude body of a dead baby lodged against the sewer wall, with eyes closed and hands clenched, its mouth open as though in a protesting cry. The small human form represents, even more impressively than the animal symbol, the callous cruelty of an economic system in which natural regard for the young and the helpless has been stifled and where life is destroyed at birth.

As can be observed from such representative illustrations, Mr. Wright's technique is a natural outgrowth of his preoccupation with theme. Although Richard Wright experimented, as do all literary craftsmen, with various forms, the reader will not find in this great writer the intricacy and subtlety of style displayed by those who came after him. But such devices as most effectively convey his ideas are repeatedly employed. The repetition, however, rarely becomes monotonous or tiring; in Richard Wright technique seldom distracts or engages our attention for its own sake, as in the case of more sophisticated writers. Rather it is almost invariably subordinated to those compelling ideas which it conveys.

NATIVE SON

THEMES. Like that other naturalistic novel with which it is most frequently compared, Theodore Dreiser's *An American Tragedy*, Richard Wright's *Native Son* is concerned with the failure of society to provide for one of its own members the benefits it has taught him to desire, and with its relentless punishing of that member for his violation of the law which has never afforded him protection. But Richard Wright's novel goes beyond Dreiser's in its indictment of the American system, for while Clyde Griffiths, the white hero of the earlier novelist's work, suffers from economic deprivation and social discrimination, Bigger Thomas, Wright's protagonist, bears the added burden of blackness in a society which automatically denies him opportunity for betterment on grounds of racial inferiority.

Added, then, to the theme of society's injustice toward a native son is that of racial conflict, involving not only the blatant persecution of Bigger by admitted racists but the wounds inflicted on his pride and his personality by those white persons who try to help him. Still another dominant theme is the elemental force within Bigger himself which drives him to behavior he can neither understand nor control. And the theme of society's failure in its dealings with Bigger subsumes two other failures, that of a Christianity which cannot save Bigger because he has never seen its principles put into actual practice, and that of a capitalistic system which excludes him from both the competition and the material rewards of which it boasts. Finally, *Native Son* treats the achievement of personal freedom through self-knowledge.

TECHNIQUES. Richard Wright's gift of image-making is displayed in full power in *Native Son*. As in his other fiction, every variety of sensory image is employed, but most striking are the visual and the auditory, the latter frequently achieving an onomatopoetic effect, as in the opening sentence, which reproduces the prolonged, metallic ring of a cheap alarm clock. Indeed, metallic imagery recurs throughout, as the hard, unyielding quality of Bigger's environment becomes more and more apparent. Visually the predominant images are black and white, constantly juxtaposed, with whiteness invariably producing a sense of dread and menace.

Not only do the images evoke a sensory response, they also serve an additional purpose, that of symbolization. The most powerful symbol of the danger posed Bigger Thomas by whiteness is the snow, a fittingly organic symbol in a novel which follows the naturalistic pattern of man at the mercy of forces he cannot control. But in addition to that major symbol of whiteness there are many others, both from nature and from objects manufactured by man.

Another noteworthy technique displayed in *Native Son* is the variation in sentence structure. For much of the narrative, especially where action is rapid, and communication between Bigger and other persons is minimal, short, simple sentences in regular subject-verb order are used. But where emotional intensity and intimacy are depicted, as in Bigger's visit to Bessie Mears' room, the sentence is extended to paragraph length, the rhythm of its movement corresponding to the sexual union of the lovers. And when the author takes us into the mind of Bigger, the prolonged sentence is employed in a stream-of-consciousness effect.

When Richard Wright composed *Native Son*, he had already served a relatively extended apprenticeship, experimenting without benefit of adequate formal education but with his own innate sense of fitness strengthened by his catholic reading. Thus the novel demonstrates his generally competent and frequently brilliant literary technique.

STRUCTURE. Like the Hegelian dialectic with which Richard Wright became familiar through his Communist association, *Native Son* employs a triadic formula. The German philosopher Hegel, whose explanation of reality influenced nineteenth-century thinking and persists into the twentieth, maintained that conscious development passes repeatedly in ascending stages from thesis, the initial premise, to antithesis, its opposite, and thus, through resultant conflict into synthesis or resolution. Similarly, *Native Son* is divided into three long divisions, Books One, Two, and Three, rather than the shorter and more numerous chapters of the average novel, and the interlocking relationship among the three is made apparent on close examination. Their alliterative subtitles, "Fear," "Flight," and "Fate" respectively, become succinct expressions of Bigger Thomas's psychological development.

> COMMENT. Like any novel of enduring significance, *Native Son* can be read on more than one level. It is preeminently a gripping story, fast-paced, shocking, often brutal, which carries the reader forward by sheer momentum. Its readability is enhanced by its horror; any student who has experienced the paradoxical pleasure afforded by fright and revulsion in reading Poe's "The Black Cat" or "The Tell-Tale Heart" will experience comparable sensations here. The novel is like Poe's great tales in another way; it treats crime and its detection. Although there are no master detectives nor any mystery concerning the identity of the criminal, a certain amount of suspense is created by Bigger's own efforts at concealment of evidence and diverting suspicion toward others. But to read only for thrill and excitement would be to miss a valuable part of the reading experience. The comparison with Poe can be extended beyond surface details, for like the great nineteenth-century author, Wright delves into the mental processes of his criminal. In doing so, he takes his reader beyond horror into those higher realms of aesthetic-emotional response insisted upon by the Greek philosopher and critic Aristotle, the realms of pity and terror.
>
> There is still another level at which the serious student should and must read *Native Son*. Although thirty-one years have passed since its first publication, many of the attitudes as well as the conditions it sets forth still remain. If America is to provide for all its native sons the rights and privileges guaranteed in its Constitution, there must be increased understanding. Both white and black students whose economic and social circumstances

have protected them from hunger and humiliation need to know these privations vicariously in order to wipe them out, along with the inequities and senseless prejudices which produce them. Perhaps Bigger Thomas is a rarity today, except in those pockets of overt racism discernible in a few geographical sections of our vast country, his place having been taken by aware and dedicated young revolutionaries who voluntarily expose themselves to violence and death in order to transform an intolerable system. Nevertheless, Bigger Thomas was an actuality, a living, breathing component of the American scene not many years ago, as attested to as much by newspaper files as by Mr. Wright's own challenging essay, "How Bigger Was Born." And so it behooves all students who lay claim to even the barest knowledge of the forces which shaped, and are still shaping, the destiny of their nation, to read *Native Son* as a commentary on the sociology of twentieth-century America.

Book One: Fear

Twenty-year-old Bigger Thomas, living in a Chicago South Side tenement with his mother, sister, and younger brother, accepts a job with the wealthy Daltons as chauffeur and furnace man. When blind Mrs. Dalton enters the bedroom where Bigger has reluctantly carried Mary, her daughter, after the girl's drunken rendezvous with her Communist friend, Jan Erlone, Bigger stifles the young woman's mutterings with a pillow to escape detection. Upon discovering that she is dead, he burns her body in the basement furnace. He thrusts in the head he must sever in order to close the furnace door, and flees back to his home.

COMMENT. In establishing fear as the thesis in the dialectic concerning Bigger Thomas as a representative of the alienated black, Mr. Wright makes careful preparation for the crime. We first see the squalid conditions under which Bigger is forced to live, where males and females must automatically avert their eyes when others are dressing, since the privacy which insures ordinary decencies is missing. Too, there is a battle with a huge rat that has invaded the Thomas apartment. Later in the day when Bigger joins his friend Gus, the conversation between the two young men reveals their puzzled resentment of the white world which allows them no participation in man's exciting conquest of the elements, such as flying one of the sky-writing planes they watch wistfully from the wintry street. In a shabby poolhall which, except for the cheap movie theatres they eagerly frequent when they can scrape together the price of admission, is their only means of recreation, they withdraw to a rear room out of earshot of Doc, the black proprietor, to discuss their plan for that afternoon's robbery of a delicatessen. Here the fear of the white world and its swift retaliation on those who invade its territory and break its laws manifests itself in tension and irritability. The reader has already been informed that Bigger deliberately excluded from his full consciousness the reality of his deprivation, for fear he would kill either himself or another person. In the encounter with other young Negroes whose life situation resembles his own, the measure of his fear is further given. It impels him to a violence that is literally uncontrollable, as when, the hour set for the robbery approaching, he actually attacks his friend Gus, kicking and beating him, and eventually threatening him with his knife until Doc intervenes. It is only after Gus retreats and the other two agree that the opportune time for the robbery is gone that Bigger admits to himself his own fear, a fear of the white world which had impelled him to avert the planned incursion into it.

In such fashion, events in Bigger's day as he awaits his five-thirty appointment with Mr. Dalton highlight the intensity of Bigger's fear. His bewildered dread of the unknown white culture becomes even more apparent on his visit to the Dalton home, where the unfamiliar luxury of the surroundings reduces him to shambling posture and clumsy gestures, and the friendly overtures of the Irish servant Peggy, the impersonal philanthropic concern of blind Mrs. Dalton, and the penetrating but kindly questioning of Mr. Dalton elicit from the embarrassed young man a series of largely monosyllabic, awkwardly propitiatory replies. But his discomfort under these advances is as nothing to that which he feels in the company of Mary and Jan. The latter's open admission that he is Communist and his eager attempts to recruit the young black man for the party only arouse in Bigger the vague suspicion and fear with which he regards all "reds." And Mary's direct friendliness, in marked contrast to the perfunctory reserve he has hitherto encountered in his rare conversations with white women, leaves him at a complete loss. When Jan takes the wheel of the Dalton car, and Bigger finds himself seated between the two, he feels as though he were "between two vast white looming walls." His acute discomfort is aggravated by their insistence that he eat with them in a South Side Negro restaurant, especially after his friend Jack stares in stupefied amazement and Bessie Mears, his best girl, shies away after seeing his companions. His only relief from the misery induced by their well-intentioned behavior is to get drunk with them, but it is a short-lived relief because after Jan takes a street-car home, Bigger must escort the drunkenly incapacitated Mary to her bedroom. At this point, the author affords the reader a brief respite from steadily accelerating fear, as Bigger in momentary sexual excitation fondles the supine young white woman. But this is quickly interrupted by the terrifying entrance of Mrs. Dalton, which impels Bigger to the instinctive act of self-protection that leads to Mary's death.

But the climax of fear has not yet been reached. The reader enters into Bigger's frenzied thought processes as he makes elaborately cunning plans for diverting suspicion. His first scheme, to ship the body in a trunk to Detroit, where, he knows from her conversation with Jan, Mary intended to go for a three-day visit, entails the horrifying procedure of placing the young woman's limp body into the trunk and carrying the gruesome burden downstairs on his back. In the basement, a crescendo of fear and horror is attained. After his decision to burn the body, we watch aghast as Mary's curly head remains out of the furnace while her clothing is already ablaze. As the frantic Bigger tries vainly to push the body farther into the engulfing fire, a greater intensification of his fear and that which now encloses the reader occurs. Hearing a noise behind him, Bigger whirls to find two enormous green eyes glaring at him; Mrs. Dalton's white cat has entered the basement through the door he failed to close.

After his fearsome accuser has scampered away, Bigger

carries out the direst act in this series of fear-impelled deeds: he severs the head from the body, wraps it in the newspapers he has spread to catch the dripping blood, and puts it and the hatchet he has used in decapitation into the furnace.

The student should be aware by now of the structural unity of Book One and the intricacy which maintains it. In reading, he has been led from the abject conditions in the black protagonist's life which induce in him both a fear of that which is external to himself and that which is internal, to a relatively insignificant display of violence that adumbrates the greater violence to come, from there to explicit manifestations of threatening, fear-inducing whiteness, and finally to the inevitable outcome of Bigger's mounting fear, the killing and its ghastly aftermath. Action has built steadily to a peak; now there must ensue a reaction, or in the terminology of the dialectic we have discerned in the structure of *Native Son*, thesis must be followed by antithesis. That antithesis is supplied in Book Two: Flight.

Book Two: Flight

Bigger's grandiose scheme for collecting money through a faked ransom note collapses when one of the reporters who have flocked to the Dalton house discovers bones and an earring in the furnace ashes. Fleeing, Bigger knows he can neither leave Bessie behind nor take her with him. He kills her and throws her body down an air-shaft in a vacant building. For one more day he evades capture by hiding in empty South Side flats, but is finally forced down from the top of a water-tank by a stream from a fire-hose and dragged by his feet to the snowy street below.

COMMENT. The triadic structural pattern initiated in Book One, as Fear supplies the *dialectic thesis*, is further developed in Book Two with Flight becoming the *antithesis*. An additional utilization of the number three is discernible: the portentous events which filled one day, a winter Saturday, and assumed ever more terrifying proportions on Sunday, finally reach their cataclysmic conclusion at the end of the third, that is, on Monday night.

It is also noteworthy that the emotion of fear which dominated Book One and which leads to the flight narrated in Book Two is further explored in Book Two, so that we actually see, to use the dialectic terminology agreed upon earlier, thesis effecting antithesis.

When Bigger first wakes on Sunday morning, the room with his sleeping family has an air of unreality until it becomes actual when touched by his fear. But as he eats breakfast with his family, the reader is given an intimation of what will be more fully propounded later, that the commission of a crime, dreadful as that crime is, has given meaning to Bigger's life. The thoughts that come to him of his daring action form in some strange way a protection against the world he feared.

Further indication that Bigger's deed has liberated him from fear is seen in an encounter in the corner drugstore with Gus, Jack, and G. H. For the first time, Bigger is at ease in their presence, the tension that had goaded him into attack completely gone.

But although fear *per se* has been expelled, one fearsome vision remains, and we shall see its frequent recurrence; Bigger is constantly beset by the image of Mary's head, the dark curls matted with blood. When the horrifying picture fills his mind as he rides the street car to the Dalton home on Sunday morning, he remembers Mary's actions while living, considering them foolish and conducive to violent reaction. The student should note also at this point how careful the author is to set forth Bigger's inability to feel any sorrow for Mary, an inability stemming from the unreality with which the white girl was invested for the young black man. But even though Bigger is not yet capable of any sympathy for Mary, he recollects with intensity the fear and shame she had made him feel. And this recollection leads to an extension of the sense of fear and shame to all black people. Looking out the window of the car, Bigger sees other black people and realizes that they too have felt fear and shame stemming from their treatment by the white world. Recalling his occasional impulse in the past to attempt some union with other black people for the purpose of resisting the white force that has kept them all separate and oppressed, he feels that fear and shame might be overcome if black people would act together.

Mr. Wright's describing these vague longings for solidarity with others serves to accentuate the loneliness which is Bigger's ordinary condition. And it is that loneliness which predominates in the treatment of flight. Even when Bigger is surrounded by reporters in the basement of the Dalton home, he is alone, striving to give the answers which he feels will sustain the impression of an ignorant, clumsy Negro who would be incapable of carrying out a crime against the all-powerful white society, and who would neither understand nor approve any revolutionary organization. Thus there is no meaningful exchange between him and his questioners. Bigger's isolation from human society is pointed up when the white cat following Mrs. Dalton into the basement bounds to his shoulder and sits there while the newspaper men excitedly photograph him.

And he is horrifyingly alone at the moment the bones found in the ashes are identified as human bones. Here, of course, the pattern of flight is resumed. As the men bend over the ashes where an earring and the hatchet blade also come into view, Bigger tiptoes away, up the stairs to his room, and jumps from his window into the snow.

The solitary nature of Bigger's flight gives way briefly when Bessie joins him, taking from her meagerly furnished room the blankets and quilts they will need in their hiding places. But the student should note that any possibility of permanent companionship is quickly dispelled. The device by which the author lets the reader know that Bessie will not long accompany Bigger follows a similar pattern to that established in the larger structure; in the account of their taking refuge in an empty house, the same statement is made three times on as many pages with only slight variation. It is the stark assertion that he can neither take her with him nor leave her behind. This fearful dilemma admits of only one solution. When Bessie sleeps after love-making, Bigger kills her by pounding her head with a brick and throws her body down an airshaft.

Once again, the flight is a solitary one.

After the second murder Bigger is able to sleep, though

fitfully. Daylight wakens him. The careful reader will be aware that it is now Monday, the third day since the beginning of the story and the last segment of Bigger's flight. When a newspaper stolen from a corner drugstore supplements details of the manhunt by a map showing parts of the South Side already covered by police, Bigger calculates the rate of search and the time when the police will reach him.

Even though the pace of flight is now accelerated, Mr. Wright still permits us to share Bigger's sensations: as he assuages his hunger with a loaf of bread he daringly buys at a bakery; as he listens from empty rooms in which he finds temporary concealment to the conversations of black people exposed by his crime to the wanton savagery of white mobs; as he is momentarily attracted to the solace of his mother's religion while listening to hymns sung by a black congregation; and eventually as in a desperate stand he climbs to a snowy roof, where he succeeds in knocking one pursuer unconscious with the butt of his gun. The tension of the rooftop episode is almost unbearable, for the reader not only shares Bigger's peril from the blazing guns in the hands of white police and vigilantes, but also the snowy cold which stiffens his limbs and fingers. Taking refuge at last on the top of a water tank, Bigger reaches the end of his flight when a fire hose is turned upon him.

Following the structural analysis suggested by the Hegelian dialectic, we shall see how Fate, treated in Book Three, becomes the synthesis of Fear and Flight.

Book Three: Fate

At the inquest three days after his capture, the coroner's jury recommends that Bigger be held on a murder charge. Taken to the Dalton home he refuses to re-enact his crime, and when he sees a flaming cross being burned he tears off a wooden cross he is wearing. Although Max had entered a plea of not guilty at Bigger's arraignment, he later changes the plea to guilty. During the dramatic three-day trial Max attempts to convince the court that Bigger's crime is part of the nation's guilt, but State Attorney

Buckley's vehement denunciations prevail, and Bigger is sentenced to die on March 3rd.

> COMMENT. The triadic pattern of the overall structure is reflected in lesser details in Book Three, for three days elapse between Bigger's capture and the coroner's inquest, and the trial itself occupies three days. But of greater importance to our understanding of Richard Wright's successful utilization of structure is the synthesis achieved in the third book, when fear and flight culminate in fate.
>
> Just as we saw that fear continued into the second book, though on a different level from the first, so in Book Three there is an ultimate fear confronting Bigger, the fear of death itself. Before he can accept his death, he must make a desperate attempt to grasp the meaning of life. Although during the three days that elapsed between his capture and the coroner's inquest he had kept himself in a kind of suspended animation, refusing food and uttering no sound, the life force in him ultimately prevails and at the time of the inquest both body and mind resume their normal functions.
>
> For a brief while it appears possible that the religion he had rejected at the time of his flight might furnish the meaning he seeks. After the black minister visits him at the Cook County Morgue, the site of the inquest, and repeats the Biblical story of creation, man's fall, and his redemption through the sacrificial death of Christ, Bigger's mind is filled with mystic images, and he allows the preacher to place a wooden cross about his neck. But whatever comfort he might have found in Christianity is forever negated when its professed followers thrust before him not the crucifix of love but the flaming cross of hate. Thereafter, Bigger will have no more Christian emblems. His vehement rejection of the meaningless cross once again follows the triadic pattern we have observed, as he flings the object out of his cell three times.
>
> But if religion is to play no part in his fate, his relations with other human beings assume a measure of stability. Bigger's first revelation that white persons can feel a genuine concern for him occurs when Jan Erlone visits him during the course of the inquest.

As a matter of fact, Mr. Wright assembles all the people most directly associated with Bigger in the small room at the Cook County Morgue to which the young man has been taken after fainting when the inquest began. Some critics have objected to this as too obviously contrived, but the student should be aware that, since the story of Bigger exhibits many dramatic values, the introduction of a moving scene at this point can be justified. Certainly, when Bigger reacts successively to the presence of his family, his friends, and Mary's parents, Mr. Wright has achieved the synthesis of fear and flight which we have noted as structural. Bigger's fate is tied to that of all these other persons, and his awareness of what he has done to them transcends his self-absorption.

Almost unbearable tension is achieved, however, through the protracted conflict between Buckley, the State Attorney who is willing to play on every conceivable fear and prejudice in order to convict the young Negro, and Max, the Jewish lawyer who defends Bigger, not only because he is interested in him as a human being, but also because he sees Bigger's crimes as the inevitable outcome of American society's three-hundred-year guilt. This conflict, with its large social implications, is focalized in Bigger's own feelings, for he vacillates between daring to hope that Max may save his life and utter hopelessness at his own realization that the forces behind Buckley are stronger than the sane humanity of Max.

If Book Three is to mean more to the student than another treatment of naturalistic determinism, however, he must read its last few pages with particular care. For Buckley's victory is not total. Bigger must go to the chair, and the horror of his end is never softened, but in his last conversation with Max he comes to a comprehension of his life's meaning. And so, the Fate that has overtaken him, a Fate which will destroy his young, strong body as mercilessly as he destroyed the bodies of his victims, finds him at last a man, and a man who can send to his mother the truthful message that he is all right.

CHARACTER ANALYSIS

A criticism recurrently leveled at *Native Son* maintains that it has only *one fully realized character*, Bigger Thomas, and that Richard Wright fails to make us believe what he sketchingly tells us about all the other characters. It is not an entirely accurate assessment of the novelist's characterization, as we shall see in our examination, but it is undeniable that Bigger's is by far the most thorough depiction.

BIGGER THOMAS. Dissatisfied with his collection of short stories, *Uncle Tom's Children,* because it was the kind of book, as he put it, that readers could shed tears over and feel good about, Richard Wright was determined that his next work would be too hard for weeping. *Native Son* was such a book largely because of its protagonist. Part of the characterization is suggested by the name *Bigger*. Although the association, through rhyme, with the derisive epithet *nigger*, undoubtedly contributed to effectiveness on first publication, the long years of avoidance of that term by socially conscious persons as well as the present casual use of it by sophisticated writers and speakers have rendered such association less meaningful. But there is another connotation which will be permanently valuable. *Like any protagonist of a literary classic, the young black man whose crimes and their punishment are presented in horrifying detail is larger than life.* Such must be the case if the novel is to produce the effects desired by its author. And so we are led to see and to understand one who, for all the restrictions of his limited environment, is greater than ordinary and is appropriately named Bigger.

If a literary character is to become real to us, we must know how he looks. Mr. Wright utilizes a variety of methods in drawing his picture of the physical Bigger Thomas. We see him first as "a black boy standing in a narrow space between two iron beds," as he turns off the alarm clock in the bedroom shared by all four members of the Thomas family. Throughout the swift-paced events of Book One, details are added which let us know that Bigger is strong and innately graceful, though, from long habit he adopts a slouching, shambling posture in the presence of whites.

The most condensed description is given in the *Tribune* article Bigger reads in the Cook County Morgue. Discounting the journalistic slant which Wright reproduces so well, a slant in this case toward the brutish quality of the subject, we learn that Bigger is about five feet nine inches in height, that his skin is very black, and that he has long arms and huge, muscular shoulders. His age we know to be twenty, and additional biographical data are provided early in the novel. We meet the other three members of the Thomas family on the opening pages, and from Bigger's answers to questions put to him by Jan on the fateful Saturday evening which is to terminate in Mary Dalton's death, we learn the following: Bigger was born in Mississippi, his schooling stopped after the eighth grade because of lack of money, the father was killed in a riot in the South while Bigger was still a child, and the Thomas family had been in Chicago for some five years at the opening of the novel.

Richard Wright not only allows us to see the physical Bigger, but he takes us into the very *consciousness* of the young man until we can feel with him. The novelist does this in two ways — through Bigger's own words, which, though halting and often ungrammatical, are nonetheless revealing, and through expository and descriptive passages.

When Bigger talks freely with his friend Gus as the two young men lean against a wall and watch a sky-writing plane, his cherished but frustrated dream is expressed through his statement, "I could fly one of them things if I had a chance." And as they discuss the impossibility of accomplishment in the white-controlled world, Bigger sighs and swears, averring, "They don't let us do nothing." And when Gus reminds him that they have always known this, Bigger agrees, but insists that he cannot accustom himself to it. "Every time I think about it," he says, "I feel like somebody's poking a red-hot iron down my throat."

In contrast to that candid admission is Bigger's *guarded speech* with whites. He is at pains to convey a sense of inferior position with his "Yessum" and "Yessuh"; and his brief answers to questions are invariably phrased in such fashion as he believes his white questioner expects. Not until near the end of the novel, when Bigger has learned to trust Max, does his speech to a white person convey his actual feeling. Even then there are difficulties, stemming from the disproportion between the vast and terrifying concepts with which the young man is struggling and the limited vocabulary with which he makes his agonized attempt to articulate these concepts. But he eventually succeeds and his words are profoundly moving.

The emotional forces which drive Bigger are conveyed by other means than his words. His swift angers and his destructive impulses stemming from fear are evidenced in the opening scene when he fiercely attacks a huge rat, and the same murderous impulse is at work in him at the time his secret dread of the delicatessen robbery impels him to a vicious assault on his friend Gus. Thus his sudden rages are part of his uncontrollable nature, but they are not directly responsible for either of the murders he commits. Although he later admits to Max that Mary Dalton's behavior toward him made him hate her, it is not that hate which causes him to smother her to death, but a frantic endeavor to escape detection by her mother. Nor does anger at Bessie incite him to kill her, but the knowledge that he can neither leave her behind nor take her with him.

For all of Bigger's primal impulses and brutal reactions, there is in him none of the fiendish delight in cruelty attributed to him by Buckley, the State Attorney. The horror inherent in his disposal of Mary's body and in the decapitation affects him so strongly that he has to force himself to go through the necessary motions, fighting faintness and nausea all the while. And the vision of the white girl's severed head haunts him repeatedly. When he kills

Bessie by beating her head to a bloody pulp with a brick, he does so while she is asleep and the room is dark; the moment when he strikes a match to assure himself that she is dead is one of torture and agony for him.

Though it is Bigger's crimes and the circumstances leading to them which loom so large in the reader's consciousness, there are other facets of his character which should not be overlooked. One is his absorption in motion pictures. Because his own world is narrowly constricted, he escapes with delight into a world where wealth and beauty are commonplace and where peril is miraculously overcome.

But Bigger's fantasizing is not completely dependent upon cinematic images. When the old black preacher retells the Biblical story of Creation, vague, splendid pictures of the emergence of Earth from Chaos form in Bigger's mind, and majestic sounds come to his inner ear. And upon listening to the Reverend Hammond's account of the Fall, Bigger sees Adam and Eve walking in fear and shame, trying to cover their nakedness, while the angel with a flaming sword drives them from the Garden of Eden out into a region of suffering and death.

Such fantasies as these serve to demonstrate *Bigger's capabilities for awe and wonder and for emotions of love and compassion.* But so brief is his life and so beset by corroding agents that his highest emotions have little opportunity for development. That he is a splendid physical specimen, in spite of poverty and its attendant deprivations, is evident throughout the novel and, consequently, his love-making with Bessie has its natural joy. But nothing in his experience has inclined him toward the secure marriage Bessie craves nor the tender affection and sense of duty it would entail. Toward his mother, his sister, and his younger brother, he is, by turns, irritable or grudgingly tolerant, until his full realization in the Cook County Morgue that "his family was a part of him, not only in blood, but in spirit." Such human relationships as persons in happier circumstances take for granted Bigger never attains, but he comes nearest in regard to Jan and

Max. Jan's genuine attempt to comprehend and communicate with Bigger, the man who has killed the girl Jan loves and who has attempted to implicate Jan himself, brings to Bigger his first sense of a white man's humanity. And toward Max, who listens to what his young black client has to say and pleads his case without hope of compensation, Bigger develops the confidence and trust that a son reposes in a good father.

The student should be aware of the *complexity of Bigger's characterization*. There is no sentimentalization of his bad deeds: he steals, he lies, he schemes to extort money, and he murders. But at the same time his humanness and his potential for good are evident. He is not a rapist; indeed, his sexual behavior is that of any normal young male. Nor is he a sadist or a fiend; he derives no pleasure from cruelty and he is haunted, as we have observed before, by the horrors of his actions. He is uneducated, but intelligent and aware. His ideological consciousness is minimal; the Communist Party is, in his mind, a vaguely sinister organization toward which he can justifiably direct the suspicion of others about his own crimes. His political conscience is no more mature; although not old enough to vote legally, he admits to Max that on two occasions he lied about his age and accepted money for voting. Still, it is never Bigger himself against whom the reader feels revulsion, but the acts he commits because both his heritage and his environment have made them inevitable. And before his execution, he comes to an understanding of other people and of himself that enables him to face death with dignity and courage.

MRS. THOMAS. Though no other member of the Thomas family is so fully characterized as Bigger, neither is any one of them stereotyped. Bigger's mother is shown as a woman with a love for her children and a determination to provide for them what she deems necessary for happiness. That she manages to maintain the ordinary decencies of life in spite of squalid living conditions is made clear at the beginning of Book One when she orders the boys to turn their heads so that she can dress. Her eagerness for Bigger to accept the job with the Daltons leads her to nag him, but that nagging is the result of genuine concern for her children's welfare and not of insensitivity. Her religious faith, though simple and unreasoned, has sustained her in a life of hardship. And unlike her son who resents conditions imposed by the white world, Mrs. Thomas accepts the supposed superiority of white persons as actual. One of the most painful scenes in which she participates, painful not only to Bigger who feels shamed by the display, but also to the reader, takes place in the Cook County Morgue when the black woman kneels at Mrs. Dalton's feet, pleading for her son's life, appealing to the other woman's knowledge of a mother's feelings. Even in her abject abasement, however, some dim perception of injustice is demonstrated as she cries that Bigger has never had a chance. And her innate courtesy does not fail her even under such stress. When Mr. Dalton, adamantly refusing to intervene in the prosecution, makes a concession to her suffering and promises that the three Thomases will not be evicted, she stifles her sobs and quietly expresses her gratitude.

VERA THOMAS. Bigger's young sister emerges from the episodes in which she appears as a timid adolescent, easily frightened, eager to please, and ready to take whatever share of family responsibility is assigned her. In preparation for work which she hopes will provide her with both money and respectability, she is taking sewing lessons at a YWCA. She exercises her sisterly prerogative of correcting her older brother's manners and morals, a habit which often goads Bigger into vicious counter-attack, but she also evokes from him a genuine concern for her well-being, especially at the time of the inquest, when, in the crowded room of the Cook County Morgue, she kneels on the floor, covers her face with her hands, and sobs. Bigger is touched because she seems "so little and helpless." And that is precisely the effect she has on the reader. To Bigger, of course, she appears physically small at that moment, but there is another sense in which the littleness of Vera is meaningful. The conditions under which she lives render her an infinitesimal part of society, a society which has no interest in her as an individual. Even the sewing lessons which offered her, at least in her confused imagination, an opportunity to make something of herself are cut short when the other members of the class taunt her with Bigger's crime. And so the last glimpse we have of Vera, as Jan leads the weeping girl from the room, confirms our impression of her as an adolescent whose dreams of a better life will never be realized, not because she lacks potential but because the system in which she lives refuses to acknowledge her existence as a human being.

BUDDY THOMAS. Bigger's little brother is a very different kind of person from his sister. His aggressive nature is made clear in the opening pages of *Native Son* as he willingly helps his older brother kill the rat which threatens their safety. And his fierce championing of Bigger, who is patently his hero and his model, causes him to rebuke Vera and defy Mrs. Thomas for what Buddy senses as their unwarranted scolding. There is further indication of Buddy's adoration when Bigger returns home after disposing of Mary's body. On Sunday morning, Buddy eagerly inquires about the new job, the make of car which Bigger is driving, and the possibility of Bigger's finding the same kind of work for him. His acquiescence in his brother's right to come and go as he pleases is manifested by his prompt agreement with Bigger's statement concerning the hour of the older boy's arrival, although Buddy knows that Bigger is lying. And his conviction of Bigger's superiority is reflected in his flat statement, after casually remarking that Bessie had been talking about marriage, that Bigger can "get a better gal" than that.

As in the case of Vera, the reader has to form his idea of Buddy's appearance from brief suggestions rather than detailed description. One such suggestion is offered as Bigger looks at Buddy, comparing and contrasting him to Jan, and finds that the younger boy looks "aimless" and "lost," "like a chubby puppy."

In spite, however, of the formlessness of Buddy's character, some traits are definable, among them an unshakable loyalty to his older brother. When Bigger leaves the Thomas home on Sunday morning, Buddy follows him down the steps, proffering the roll of bills Bigger had dropped, and asks if he can help. Knowing that Bigger could not have come by that much money in an honest fashion, he is uncritical and readily accedes to Bigger's injunction to tell no one. In addition to loyalty, Buddy possesses courage. When the Thomas family visits Bigger at the Cook County Morgue, the small boy exhibits none of the weeping timorousness of his mother and sister but stoutly declares for all to hear that Bigger should tell him if he is being falsely accused so that he can get a gun and kill four or five of his brother's tormentors. Nor do his mother's sobbing admonitions silence him; he continues to encourage Bigger with such words as are at his command.

Thus, although the reader's acquaintance with the small boy is limited, Buddy becomes memorable for his fidelity and his fearlessness.

BESSIE MEARS. The most outstanding quality of the girl who furnishes Bigger with his only peace but whom he must kill because he can neither leave her behind nor take her with him is her sense of being lost. She is aware that she is lost and refers to the fact more than once. The inevitability of her destruction is, of course, most fully apparent in the horror of her death, compounded by the disclosure at the inquest that she did not, as Bigger hoped, die at once even after the bludgeoning, but made a feeble, frantic effort to escape from the shaft into which she was thrown. But the circumstances of her life are such that, even if she had lived longer, there could have been no happiness for her.

We first see Bessie in Ernie's Kitchen Shack where Bigger has taken Mary and Jan at Mary's insistence. At this point her capability for gayety is demonstrated as the music of an automatic phonograph plays and she laughs into Bigger's face. But for most of the time there is little gayety in Bessie's life. Working long hours in a white family's kitchen, seven days a week with only Sunday afternoons off, she spends the little spare time she has in a frenetic attempt to compensate for her habitual drudgery. And the greater part of that compensation comes through drinking. When Bigger provides her with the liquor she must have, she allows him to make love to her. Casual as their love-making appears, however, there is great tenderness in her so that what she gives Bigger is more than physical release. When her two soft palms hold his face, the shame and fear he experiences in the world outside leave him for a while and he experiences peace.

Bessie's dearest wish is that of most girls her age. She wants very much to be married and to have the security she feels marriage would bring her. The fate which is hers is in sharp contrast to what she desires. Adding to her misery is her keen awareness of her situation. That awareness is fully expressed through her words to Bigger immediately before they leave her room for the last time. She does not actually know that Bigger will kill her, but she does know that her life is now hopeless. With hands clenched and with tears gushing from her eyes, she rocks to and fro in anguish as she wails that all her life has been full of trouble, and that she has never bothered anybody but always worked hard every day for as long as she can remember, until she was tired enough to drop, and then she had to get drunk to forget and to sleep.

The reader is even more moved by the absence of fulfillment for Bessie than for Vera because Bessie is no mere slip of a girl, but a fully developed young woman with all a woman's responses and dreams. Through her speech, her actions, and also through Bigger's eyes, we see and know her quite clearly, and our pity for her unfulfilled life is exceeded only by our horror at her bloody and prolonged death.

REVEREND HAMMOND. Although the Negro preacher who urges Bigger to accept the consolation and redemption of the Christian faith and who places around the young man's neck a chain with a wooden cross appears only briefly, he is a distinct personality. He is described as tall and well-dressed, his suit being jet-black. Calling on the accused man at Mrs. Thomas's request, he offers the comfort of an orthodox Christianity, and his speech, the dialectal features of which are reproduced by the novelist's characteristic compound of phonetic spelling and word arrangement, demonstrates his understanding both of that Christianity and the human beings he serves.

As the minister exhorts Bigger to think only of the state of his soul and to throw himself on God's mercy, he reminds the young black man that only the soul, which is completely independent of skin color, belongs to God. In order to impress on his listener the ineffable nature of man's relation to his Maker he retells the Genesis story of Creation and of the Fall of Man, concluding his impassioned exhortation with a simplified but theologically sound summary of Atonement, that is, the sacrificial death of the Son of God to insure man's being forgiven.

The student should note that *the characterization of this black pastor is neither stereotyped nor pejorative.* Bigger himself eventually rejects both Reverend Hammond's ministrations and the religion he represents, but the young Negro's rejection is not occasioned by anything the older man does or says but by the failure of a so-called Christian society to manifest the mercy it professes to believe in.

The Reverend Hammond's own practice of the virtues of love and forgiveness which he enjoins upon others is shown by his visit to Bigger and also by his enthusiastic commendation of Jan, after the latter has declared his freedom from hatred. But the black minister's acceptance of human solidarity does not extend to any tolerance of Jan's political philosophy. On the contrary, when the older man feels that Jan is urging Communistic ideas, he intervenes, insisting that, although he respects Jan's feelings, the course he advocates will only stir up more hate. To Jan's reply that Bigger must fight for people's understanding, the Reverend Hammond declares his agreement with the young white man's desire to change men's hearts but reiterates his opposition to any course of action which will "stir up mo' hate." When Jan inquires how it is possible to change men's hearts with newspapers "fanning hate into them every day," the minister falls back on a simple reliance on Divine power, stoutly asserting that God can change them. Thus, there is in the minister none of the more sophisticated perception of analogies between religious ideals and political action that characterizes many members of the clergy.

What Reverend Hammond lacks in sophistication, however, he makes up for in consistency of action, practicing a steadfast persistence even in the face of physical attack. When Bigger throws the wooden cross through the door of his cell in the Cook County Jail, the old preacher, faithfully carrying out the New Testament injunction to visit those in prison, quietly picks it up and starts into the cell. And even after Bigger has slammed the door with such force that the old man is knocked down, Reverend Hammond rises slowly, picks up his hat, his Bible and the cross which Bigger has flung away, and sorrowfully consigning his young charge to God, drops the cross back into the cell before walking away.

A mark of Richard Wright's novelistic greatness is his ability to present with sympathy even those characters whose beliefs are not his own. Like Bigger, Mr. Wright found institutionalized Christianity inadequate, but toward its sincere adherents he displays understanding and respect. Reverend Hammond is a simple man, but strong and good.

MARY DALTON. In creating the character of the young white woman who becomes, almost by accident, the victim of murder, Richard Wright was confronted with a *literary problem*: how to make the murdered girl real and believable without diverting the reader's attention from the murderer, who is after all, the major character. To develop her character completely would be to run the risk of evoking from the reader the kind of sympathy which Mr. Wright shows State Attorney Buckley arousing in those who have no personal knowledge of this wealthy girl. On the other hand, to dismiss her casually as a human link in the chain of circumstances that binds Bigger to his fate would be to display a shocking callousness, detrimental to the very purpose of this novel, which, among other things, makes a plea for the value of human life. *The problem is solved successfully. Mary Dalton becomes real without completely absorbing the reader's attention.*

The twenty-three-year-old daughter of a philanthropic Chicago millionaire is a physically attractive young woman. She is described as small, and looking to Bigger "like a doll in a show window, with black, curly hair and black eyes." Her independent, rebellious nature is demonstrated when, upon her first encounter with Bigger, she asks the young black man in her father's presence whether he belongs to a union, and lightly taunts Mr. Dalton for being a capitalist.

Further proof of Mary's unconventional ideas and behavior is offered by the Irish servant Peggy, who informs a shocked and incredulous Bigger that Mary runs around with "reds." Peggy finds some mitigation of this questionable association in Mary's feeling sorry for people and believing that the "reds" can help, but sadly admits that Mary is "wild."

Confirmation of Peggy's assessment comes quickly, when Bigger is ordered by the young white woman not to drive her to the University as she had first told him to do, but to the Loop, and is further instructed to lie about the drive if questioned. And after they are joined by Jan Erlone, Mary's behavior further demonstrates her rejection of prejudiced convention, as Jan and she insist that Bigger accompany them to Ernie's Kitchen Shack and join their table.

Mary's "wildness" is also illustrated by her excessive drinking. We see that intoxication is not unusual for her, as her mother reveals that Mary has come home drunk previous to the night Bigger has to assist her to her room.

An additional facet of Mary's character is seen in her well-meaning but insensitive treatment of Bigger. Her attempts at friendliness carry with them an assault on Bigger's personal dignity and his right to his own privacy. When Mary flatly asserts that she has never been in a Negro home and does not really know how Negroes live, Bigger feels both shame and fear, translated into hatred, as he admits later to Max.

Mary Dalton, then, whose principal role in *Native Son* is as the victim of an unpremeditated, and indeed accidental, murder, is neither so fully characterized as to distract attention from Bigger nor so flatly depicted as to acquire no personality save as a type. Rather, she emerges from Mr. Wright's treatment as an attractive, well-intentioned young white woman who lacks both self-discipline and a real awareness of other people's humanness.

MR. DALTON. Henry Dalton, Mary's multi-millionaire father, displays somewhat more sensitivity in his conversation with Bigger than his daughter. However, his flaw is seen as a kind of paternalism. Although he establishes boys' clubs on the South Side in a philanthropic endeavor to provide wholesome recreation for underprivileged black youth, and although he makes an attempt at individual rehabilitation by employing young Negroes who, like Bigger, may have had difficulties with school authorities and law-enforcing officials, he does so without personal sacrifice and with a minimum of personal involvement. Nor has he developed any genuine understanding of economic and social conditions.

Living in luxury on fashionable Drexel Boulevard, Mr. Dalton, ironically, owns the South Side Real Estate Company to which the Thomas family pays eight dollars a week for their one rat-infested room in a miserable tenement on Indiana Avenue. Furthermore, Mr. Dalton conforms to the discriminatory practices which make it impossible for boys like Bigger ever to develop to their full potential, for he rents to Negroes only in the areas set aside for them, making no effort to provide more comfortable housing for them elsewhere. In addition, he charges Negro tenants higher rent than he charges whites whose dwellings are in much better condition. When pressed by Max at the Coroner's inquest as to his reasons for acceding to such unjust conditions, he can only reply, lamely, that it is the custom to rent to Negroes only in restricted areas, and that he feels that Negroes are happier with their own kind.

It should be observed, however, that Mr. Dalton is not presented as a willfully cruel man nor a pronounced racist. His dealings with Bigger before the murder are courteous and amiable, and even under the stress of the inquest he promises Mrs. Thomas protection against eviction. And yet his very virtues condemn him.

Educated, well-bred, and wealthy, he has a moral responsibility toward his fellow-man that goes beyond the exercise of a benevolent philanthropy, the responsibility to change the system which has provided his millions so that opportunity for development is provided every "native son." He has evaded that responsibility. The palliative measures he substitutes for reform are pointed up when he insists at the inquest that he has no bitterness and offers as proof of his clemency that he had that very day sent "a dozen ping-pong tables to the South Side Boys' Club." Boris Max, Bigger's lawyer, responds with a vehemence that rejects such irrelevancy, "My God, man! Will ping-pong keep men from murdering?"

MRS. HENRY DALTON. Perhaps because Mrs. Dalton is present at the murder of Mary, and also because we view her consistently through Bigger's eyes, the multi-millionaire's blind wife presents a menacing quality. The fifty-three-year-old woman is, we learn, a retired school teacher and we observe from her remarks that, like her husband, she wishes to treat Negroes in a charitable manner. But her very appearance inspires dread in Bigger. She is tall and thin, and both her face and hair are completely white. Bigger first sees her walking silently, with her long white fingers touching the walls on either side of her as she makes her sightless way into the room.

That she loves her rebellious daughter is unquestionable. Her concern is revealed by her actions and speech in Mary's room the night of the murder. Her wounded pride is shown by her discovery, through the smell of alcohol, that the young woman is drunk. And her religious bent is indicated when she kneels by her daughter's bed to pray.

The intensity of her anguish at her daughter's death is brought out at the inquest, when, as she fumbles with the earring found in the furnace ashes and displayed as evidence, her shoulders shake with her weeping. But she is able to compose herself and to answer questions which not only establish Mary's ownership of the pair of earrings, one of which now mutely accuses the girl's murderer, but reveal a strong sentimental attachment, for the jewelry had been given Mrs. Dalton by her mother when she reached eighteen, just as the woman had, at the same age, been given them by her mother. This testimony helps also to characterize Mrs. Dalton as the inheritor of a stable family tradition in contrast to the shifting and precarious circumstances of the Thomas family.

Like her husband, Mrs. Dalton continues to disclaim any ill will toward Negroes in general. But the absence in her, as in him, of any genuine understanding of a black person, is exhibited at the moment when Mrs. Thomas, to Bigger's unbearable shame, abases herself before the white woman and frantically implores her to intervene. Making no equation between her own feelings at the loss of a child and Mrs. Thomas's, Mrs. Dalton touches the other mother's head, calmly admonishing her to think of her other children, averring that she herself had done all possible by consenting to Bigger's employment and that the matter is out of her hands.

The student will find that Mr. Wright has provided the clue to Mrs. Dalton's character in her physical disability. This wealthy white woman who appears superficially as a paragon of rectitude and benevolence, is, on another level, actually the grave threat to others that she seems to Bigger, for *her blindness is more than physical.* She is incapable of seeing the yearning aspirations and the desperate needs of other human beings.

JAN ERLONE. One of the two most sympathetic characterizations of white persons in the novel is that of Jan Erlone, Mary Dalton's friend. An enthusiastic and idealistic young organizer for the Communist party, he is distrusted not only by the elder Daltons and their servant Peggy but also initially by Bigger, whose distaste for "reds" is not lessened by Jan's friendly advances at their first meeting. Indeed, Bigger does not hesitate to implicate the young white man in his own crime, and only gradually do Jan's honest efforts to understand and to help the person who has injured him so deeply transform Bigger's hostility into trust and love.

Jan is described as a physically attractive person, with blond hair, blue eyes, and a kind face. His character traits, revealed through his behavior and his words, are also appealing to the reader. His casually courteous treatment of Bigger at their first encounter indicates that he makes no artificial distinctions among human beings. And that he is a young man in love becomes clear as Bigger drives the other two, at Mary's request, through Washington Park. The girl rests easily in Jan's arms and Bigger can see the two kissing as he occasionally looks into the rear view mirror. Thus, the intensity of Jan's grief at Mary's death is obvious, and we feel sympathy for him in that grief.

But the most memorable quality in this young man is his freedom from racial prejudice and his human compassion. The effect of his words and his attitude on Bigger are best displayed at the time of the inquest. When Jan first enters the room where Bigger has been taken after collapsing, Bigger's first thought is that the white man has come for revenge. But as Jan tells him of how he has come to understand why the young black man whom he tried to befriend hated him, because of what white men had done to Negroes, and of how his own impulsive anger against Mr. Dalton and then against Bigger had made him want to kill, Bigger listens in bewilderment. When Jan recounts his realization that if he killed, the dreadful cycle of events would never stop, and asserts that his own suffering has led him to see deeper into other men, Bigger begins to understand. And after Jan has disavowed anger and hatred and has made his offer to help through bringing a lawyer, Bigger does begin to trust him. To express the transformation effected in Bigger's thinking by this declaration of friendship from a white man, Mr. Wright uses a phrase from the New Testament, where, in the opening chapter of the Gospel of John, the Incarnation, the bodily form taken by the Son of God for the sake of sinful men, is announced very simply: "The word became flesh." This is not to say that Jan is a Christ figure; the attribution to one character of such sacrificial and divine attributes as parallel those associated with the New Testament Christ was a frequent occurrence in novels written around the time of *Native Son,* but Richard Wright does not create such a figure.

Rather, as applied to Jan, the Biblical phrase simply expresses the effect upon Bigger of seeing a white man as a human being.

Jan Erlone, then, whom we see as a young man dedicated to an ideology but at the same time capable of enjoying the normal pleasures of eating and drinking and of loving an attractive girl, undergoes, through mistreatment and bereavement, a *development into a wiser and more compassionate person*. Thus he serves as the embodiment of the deeply human qualities Bigger had so sorely needed — acceptance of another's personality, total honesty in intercourse, and genuine concern for the other's well-being.

BORIS A. MAX. The second white character who is sympathetically presented is the Communist lawyer whom Jan brings to Bigger, Boris A. Max.

Max is described as a tall, silver-haired man with a lean white face, keen gray eyes, a voice "quiet, but kind," and a faint smile about his lips. Like his black client, Boris A. Max knows what it is to be hated, for he is not only from the Labor Defenders and thus the object of distrust and suspicion, he is also a Jew. But, as he makes clear to Bigger, he is not embittered by the hatred of others, and he knows how to fight the unreason and ignorance which engender such hatred.

Max's assured legal knowledge and his mastery of tactics are constantly in evidence. From the moment Bigger accepts his offer to represent him, he protects his client's interests and insists upon his rights. No irregularity on Buckley's part, no attempt of the State Attorney to appeal to emotion rather than to present evidence, is left unchallenged. Nor is any possible means of defending Bigger overlooked. And even when Max's eloquent courtroom plea has failed and Bigger is sentenced to die, the persistent lawyer does not give up, but appeals directly to the Governor, going in person to ask for clemency.

It is not only the mastery of his profession and his unflagging zeal on behalf of his client which distinguishes Max, but also his psychological insight. His probing questions, both at the time of the inquest and later in Bigger's cell in the Cook County Jail, elicit from the young Negro an articulation of his hopes and dreams, as well as his frustrations and rages, that no other human being has ever effected. The student will recall that in response to Mr. Dalton's interrogation, during the interview before Bigger was employed, the young man gave the answers he felt were expected. But to the incisive yet sympathetic questions put to him by the Jewish lawyer whom he has come to trust, Bigger opens his heart.

The episodes which contribute further to the reader's knowledge of Boris A. Max are the trial and the last visit to Bigger before his execution. Rather than attempting the impossible feat of disproving the murder and freeing Bigger, Max enters a plea of guilty, and then endeavors to save his client's life through an argument against the death penalty. Nor does he resort to sentimentality as he might well have done by utilizing the squalid conditions under which Bigger had lived and the pathetic deprivations of the Thomas family in order to arouse pity in his listeners. Rather, Max uses his command of logic and of words to convince the Court that Bigger's crime was part of a very way of life resulting from the enslavement of hundreds of thousands of people for more than two hundred years, an enslavement which ended only when machines made it economically impossible, and the subsequent denial to those who had been enslaved of any share of the wealth they had helped create. He argues that the demand for Bigger's death stems from the guilt-feelings of those who share this way of life, and that the only way to reverse the cycle of hate and fear and violence, which may at some point erupt into a far bloodier civil war than that which technically freed American slaves, is to choose life and not death. To send Bigger to prison, he asserts, rather than to execute him, would be to affirm life and to uphold two basic concepts of American civilization: "personality and security — the conviction that the person is inviolate and that which sustains him is equally so."

At the conclusion of his speech, Max's appearance, with his eyes tired and sunken, reveals how much of himself has gone into it. But even his failure to avert the death sentence does not terminate his efforts to aid the person whose worth as a human being this wise, compassionate man recognizes without any minimizing of the horror of his crime. Although later in his cell Bigger turns his face to the wall, Max still proffers comfort and hope through his promise to see the Governor.

As the reader knows, that final effort to save Bigger's life fails. But once more Max goes to his young friend in his jail cell, on the last day of the doomed man's life. And now it is Bigger who puts questions to Max, questions whose urgency the older man does not at first comprehend, because in his weariness and his grief for the condemned murderer he is attempting to soothe and comfort rather than instruct. But as Bigger persists in his desperate attempt to learn more about life before death puts an end to it, Max accepts the almost unbearable demand, catching Bigger's shoulders in a tight grip before sinking back on the cot. And when the young black man, overcome by the anticipation of his electrocution, runs to the steel door of the cell and shakes the bars, Max once again takes him by the shoulders and then responds to Bigger's agonized question as to whether those who hated him and sent him there to die were also striving for something as he himself had been. His face ashy from emotional strain, Max beckons Bigger to the window and placing his arm once again around Bigger's shoulders points out the buildings in the Loop, asserting that it is the belief and faith of men that keeps the buildings as a *metaphor* of human aspiration and achievement; he then *allegorizes* the circumstances that have brought Bigger to his dread fate as a few men squeezing the buildings so tightly in their hands that other men's dreams are crushed. In their fear of losing what they have, the owners, says Max, push other men down into the mud. Then, in anger, those who have been pushed out try to re-enter the buildings and some, like Bigger, kill. That, says Max, is not the way to restore the buildings. At this point, his voice falters at the painful admission that it is now too late for Bigger to work with others who are trying "to make the world live again." No longer able to look into the young man's questioning eyes, Max closes his own as he utters a bald statement of Bigger's imminent death and then urges him to die free, understanding other men and believing in himself.

The method of Max's departure from the cell reveals his anguish. With eyes wet, he extends his hand to Bigger, and although he is able to say good-bye quietly, he gropes for his hat like a blind man. Once outside he stands for a moment. The trust he has inspired in his client does not falter, as Bigger sends his last message to the living, a request for Max to "tell Jan hello." And once again, the older man and the younger bid each other good-bye.

Though Max's brilliance, professional excellence, and compassionate nature are established shortly after he is introduced into the narrative, Mr. Wright has added still another dimension to his character in the episode above — Max's *poetic power to translate abstract truth into concrete images*. If the student will carefully re-read the *parable* of the buildings, the full effectiveness of which cannot be conveyed by any paraphrase, he will be struck by the beauty and truth of the Jewish lawyer's words. *In characterizing Boris A. Max, Mr. Wright has succeeded in investing him with the qualities of a Hebrew prophet.*

BUCKLEY. Richard Wright's characterization of the other white lawyer who plays a major role in Bigger's fate is in sharp contradistinction to that of Max. The State's Attorney embodies so many of the qualities informed readers have come to associate with the opportunist who deliberately plays on men's prejudices and fears for his own aggrandizement that the student may first think of him as a *stock figure* and dismiss him. It should be remembered, however, that when *Native Son* was first published, awareness of *Buckley's type* was not so widespread as now, and it was part of Mr. Wright's purpose to make his readers aware of such a figure. Furthermore, there are occasional details which give this white lawyer a distinctive personality.

We learn some important facts about Buckley before we actually see him. In the first book, *Fear*, Bigger, killing time before his afternoon appointment, sees men across the street pasting a poster to a signboard, and recognizes the face as that of Buckley, who is running for State's Attorney. After the workers drive away in their truck, Bigger looks at the poster again, noting that the fleshy white face is stern and that the index finger of one hand points straight at each passer-by. The lettering of the poster also helps to characterize Buckley: all in caps it says, "If You Break the Law, You Can't Win." The simplistic approach to the complex matter of legality is calculated to remind viewers that the man pictured there is on the side of law, and thus to aid in the winning of his election. Bigger rightly assesses motives when he mumbles at the pictured face, "You let whoever pays *you* off win!"

The initial impression of Buckley is deepened when Bigger actually encounters him at the coroner's inquest. Here we learn more about his appearance; he is tall and gray-eyed. Both his words and gestures reveal him as a blustering bully; in verbal sparring with Max he refers to Bigger in the latter's presence as "scum." And in his direct dealing with the young Negro he is even more insulting. He walks about the room with his hat on the back of his head, then pauses at Bigger's cot, and towering over him, addresses him repeatedly as "boy," the most belittling term a white man can employ toward a black.

As Buckley persists in his eventually successful effort to force a signed confession from the murderer, he uses every possible means to intimidate and entrap the young Negro. We have already noted that Bigger at this point refuses to implicate anyone else, to admit to crimes which he did not commit, or to take advantage of Buckley's cunning suggestion that, if the young man will only tell him everything, the State's Attorney will see that he is "sent to the hospital for an examination." Bigger's angry repudiation of the last offer arises from the Negro's knowledge that he is not insane and his unwillingness to be called so. But Buckley's tender of the possibility is occasioned by no compassion nor even any belief that Bigger will thus escape death, but only by his determination to secure a signed confession. And when the black man sees the futility of further resistance and tells exactly what he did on the fateful night as a stenographer takes down his every word and then, hand shaking, signs the paper, Buckley's comment is indicative of the half-knowledge which makes men like him so successful in their dealings with helpless people, "Just a scared colored boy from Mississippi."

Although Buckley's behavior so far has revealed to us almost all of his characteristics, a further look at this despicable man during the actual trial will further demonstrate the kind of egocentric person he is. In the first place, he has dressed carefully for the role he is preparing to play; he is wearing a black suit and there is a tiny pink flower in his coat lapel. In the second place, he deliberately uses emotionally-charged words to arouse his listeners, not to any sense of common humanity with shared conditions, as Max had attempted to do, but to fear for their own security and hatred for one who threatens it. The pejorative terms Buckley applies to the black defendant merit the reader's careful attention: "this black mad dog," "this sly thug," "this hardened black thing," "this rapacious beast." Finally, his willingness to invoke a Deity whose name will assure listeners of the lawyer's own alignment with respectable religion is revealed in his final appeal to the judge for Bigger's conviction, an appeal made "in the name of Almighty God." Thus, as we hear his booming voice and watch him wiping his red face as newsmen scramble for the door, we know, as does Bigger, that the Negro will have to die. We also know that Buckley, through his deliberate manipulation of human feelings and his wickedly skillful showmanship, has made his own re-election to public office certain.

OTHER CHARACTERS. Although no other person in the novel is so strongly characterized as those whom we have just discussed, there are a number who not only perform an essential function in the working out of the story, but who are endowed, in greater or lesser degree, with *individualizing traits* by the novelist. Among other black characters whom the reader is likely to remember are Bigger's three friends, Gus, G. H., and Jack. Deprived like Bigger of satisfactory means of self-fulfillment, they too have turned to petty crime. But the fierce resentment that impels Bigger to his destructive behavior is not so strong in them, and the spirit of mimicry and parody which can make life endurable is particularly notable in Gus, who enters with Bigger into a game they frequently enjoy, playing "white," that is, the acting out of brief scenes in which they impersonate such white celebrities as J. P. Morgan, the famous financier, or the President of the United States. Other facets of their personalities are evident, as when Gus reveals his understanding that it is Bigger's own fear which prompts him to taunt his friends, or Jack's eager curiosity concerning the sexual exploits of wealthy employers, and the pleasure he derives from his humorous speculation that rich people do not even have to turn over in their sleep because a butler stands by their beds at night and gently rolls them over whenever he hears them sigh. And their loyalty to their friend, however much that quality is intermingled with apprehension and embarrassment, is displayed by their visits to him at the time of the inquest and later in his jail cell.

Another Negro character is Doc, the proprietor of the poolroom where the four young men find momentary relaxation and where they plan their minor burglaries. A fat man whom we see holding "a half-smoked, unlit cigar in his mouth" as he leans on the counter, Doc is regarded with some respect by his young customers, as is evident by their caution not to let him overhear their plotting. Too, his realistic appraisal of his environment and of those who are its product is manifested at the time Bigger makes his unwarranted attack on Gus. Doc reaches behind the counter for his gun, and when the frenzied Bigger cuts the green cloth of the billiard table, he angrily orders the young man out. But the fact that he does no bodily harm in his anger stems as much from his reluctance to inflict harsh punishment on the young black whose repressive environment he shares as from his weary knowledge of the lengths to which Bigger might go.

There are two other Negroes whom we encounter only briefly and whose names we learn as Bigger, in hiding, listens to their conversation from a vacant room in a two-story flat building. That one of them has the same name as Bigger's young friend Jack seems natural enough, since the name is an ordinary one. The argument ensuing between Jack and the other man, Jim, concerns what they would do with Bigger if they should encounter him. Jack insists, to Jim's dismay, that he would turn the fugitive over to his white pursuers to avoid any further trouble for himself. He angrily accuses Bigger of causing him to lose his job, saying that he was turned off because his white employer thought all Negroes were like Bigger. His own method, he says, is to get along with people so that he can take care of his wife and children. He considers any defiance of white people an insane act, because, as his shortsighted practicality tells him, there are so many more whites than blacks that the former could easily destroy the latter. Jim, on the other hand, avers that he would die rather than give Bigger up. He reminds Jack that every Negro looks guilty to white pursuers, and to Jack's complaint that actions like Bigger's "stir up trouble," he retorts that it is whites who are stirring up trouble at this point, beating Negroes all over the city. And he also points out that being a good man is no protection if one belongs to a group under attack, and that blacks must fight for their rights.

The student may feel, and with some justification, that *the conversation between these two is introduced primarily for the purpose of heightening Bigger's sense of danger even from other Negroes.* But Mr. Wright's unerring transcription of speech confers a recognizable individuality even on those who appear briefly.

One additional Negro character deserves attention, although he remains nameless, the insane man placed temporarily in Bigger's cell, a brown-skinned man of about Bigger's size, with bloodshot eyes and flecks of saliva on his lips. We learn the nature of his psychosis from his own shouted accusations and from an explanation which another prisoner gives to Bigger. The man has been studying at the university and trying to write a book on economic and social conditions among Negroes. Breaking under the strain, he now believes that his data have been stolen and that his university professor had him arrested. Convinced that he has arrived at the real truth of the treatment of Negroes, he plans to tell his findings to the President of the United States so that conditions will be changed. That morning he had been picked up in the lobby of the Post Office in his underwear, waiting to see the President. Before he is taken out of Bigger's cell in a strait-jacket, he screams that he will tell the President of the crowded conditions on the South Side, of the half-spoiled food that Negroes are forced to buy, of the inadequate hospital care, and of schools so crowded that they breed perverts. It might be argued that this nameless man is more a *mouthpiece for the novelist* than he is a believable person, but Bigger's increasing fear of him makes us, too, feel him as a tangible danger. The truth of his charges outweighs the unreason of his attempt to right the wrongs he has uncovered, and his demented behavior reminds us that intolerable living conditions may push a sensitive person over the line dividing the sane from the insane.

There remain for our consideration a few white characters, none of whom plays so important a part in Bigger's fate as the three Daltons and the two attorneys, but each of whom, in greater or less degree, contributes to our understanding. The first of these is Peggy, the middle-aged Irish servant in the Dalton home. A kindly woman, without any overt racism, she nonetheless shares her employers' tendency to substitute philanthropy for social justice, informing Bigger, during their first conversation, that Mr. Dalton has done a great deal for "your people," changing the phrase, at Bigger's puzzled question, to "colored people."

Far less sympathetic is the characterization of Britten, the private investigator employed by Mr. Dalton. The menace he represents for Bigger is objectified by the shining badge on his chest which he displays before questioning the frightened young man in the Dalton basement before the discovery of Mary's body. And though he assures Bigger with false heartiness that he is not "the law," he uses the same tactics in his interrogation which we see on a larger scale employed by Buckley at the inquest. Both words and actions reveal the detective as contemptuous of black people and hostile toward any political deviation. When Jan is summoned to the Dalton home, after Bigger has lied about the young white man's actions the night before, Britten subjects him, though with less success, to the kind of bullying inquisition he had directed at Bigger. And later, after Bigger has delivered his kidnap note, Britten tells the reporters he is sure of Jan's guilt, because "these reds'll do anything."

The reporters who swarm into the Dalton house are scarcely distinguishable from each other, but their effect on Bigger characterizes them as a group. The young Negro, watching them move about the basement with their hats on and smoking cigars or cigarettes, senses a coldness in them toward everyone and an attitude as of participants in a sport. Their determination to secure news by any available means is evidenced by the attempt of one to bribe Bigger. And their preoccupation with their stories is reflected in a remark by one that he will slant his writing "toward the primitive Negro" who shuns white civilization. In the course of this conversation Bigger's assessment of their predatory instincts is verified by the words of another who exclaims that this is "better than Loeb and Leopold." The student, remembering the actual murder carried out by those two, will note that the adjective *better* applied to a horrifying crime demonstrates that these are men who measure any and all human behavior according to its news value.

We observed that even during the mass reaction to the police hunt, Richard Wright briefly characterizes two Negroes whose attitudes toward Bigger are diametrically opposed. Among the white pursuers, no sympathy is manifested for Bigger or any other Negro, and mass hysteria is graphically depicted, but near the end of the chase, two white men briefly emerge as individuals. Laboriously making their way to the rooftop where Bigger crouches against a chimney, they pause for a brief dialogue before going through the trapdoor. The subject of their talk is a scantily dressed young Negro woman in one of the rooms they have searched; the man called Jerry, whom Bigger will knock unconscious once he is out on the roof, speculates idly as to why any Negro man would be interested in a white woman with such good-looking women of his own race available, to which the other replies coarsely that he would abandon the hunt if he could stay with her himself. (In this passage Wright hints at questions which Eldridge Cleaver is to study in depth, a quarter of a century later, in his *Soul on Ice*.)

There remain for our consideration only a few other white persons whose lives impinge, however briefly, on Bigger's. At his trial, Mrs. Dalton's aged mother, Mrs. Rawlson, testifies that the earring found in the furnace is one of a pair she had given her daughter. The newspapermen we saw in the Dalton home appear again to tell of the discovery of the bones in the ashes; six doctors say that Bessie was assaulted; two of Bigger's former teachers assert that though Bigger was "dull," he was sane. And culminating the array of white accusers is the judge himself. Bigger sees the Honorable Chief Justice Alvin C. Hanley entering the courtroom in long black robes and with "a dead-white face." After Max enters the plea of guilty it is Justice Hanley who explains the three eventualities to Bigger: he may be sentenced to death; he may be sent to the penitentiary for life; or he may be imprisoned for a shorter term of not less than fourteen years. And it is he who pronounces the final, irrevocable sentence against Bigger, that he shall die.

> COMMENT. Although the other characters of *Native Son* function primarily in their relation to Bigger, and thus are seen largely through his eyes, a careful observation of dialogue and of descriptive and narrative detail will convince the reader of their individuality. Furthermore, Mr. Wright has provided us with sufficient variety in characterization to increase our understanding of the American scene just prior to this country's entry into World War II. And through the completely realized characterization of Bigger himself, the reader comes into such knowledge of a human being pushed by circumstances into a hideous crime — and paying the full penalty of his crime — that the reader's own compassion, i.e., his capacity to *feel with*, is immeasurably increased.

THEMES

As in any novel worth consideration, Richard Wright's *Native Son* presents *themes of universal concern*. But because the title character is a black American, thematic content is of necessity somewhat narrowed; that is, although the novel deals ultimately with the question of the American ideal itself, our nation's failure to uphold its ideal is presented through the experience of a native son who is black. In spite of this limitation, however, the student should be aware that *all themes here encountered have applicability to Americans of whatever skin tone, and that, furthermore, this applicability can be extended to all human beings who attempt to live and work together*. There is another fact he should bear in mind as the working out of various themes is presented: *no one theme among those treated here is separate from any other*. On the contrary, the *five predominant themes* of *social injustice, racial conflict, ideology, violence as a personal necessity*, and the *achievement of human freedom* are inextricably related. Thus, as the reader encounters Mr. Wright's treatment of one of these, he will at the same time perceive that it is part of a cluster which comprises the other four.

SOCIAL INJUSTICE. Although, as has already been made clear, the novel never sentimentalizes Bigger's crime or Bigger himself, but presents with unequivocal realism each horrifying detail of the two murders he commits, *Native Son* also treats a greater crime, that of a society against one of its own. In a nation founded on the stated principle that "all men are created free and equal" and "are endowed by their Creator with unalienable rights," Bigger and his family are forced to live in squalid surroundings at the mercy of filth and vermin. Any possibility of escaping such conditions is nullified on two counts, a restrictive residential policy practiced even by those who, like Mr. Dalton, consider themselves philanthropists, and by the inadequacies of a dual educational system. Although twenty years old, Bigger has completed only eight grades of school, six in his birthplace in Mississippi, two in Chicago, where his white teachers, as is brought out at his trial, considered him "dull."

An ironic element of the social injustice to which Bigger is subjected is the denial of his most cherished wishes. Foremost among them is his dream of becoming an aviator, and of fighting for his country. At the time when the action of *Native Son* occurs, the *United States was outraged by the behavior of Fascists in Mussolini's Italy and Nazis in Hitler's Germany, and would soon be at war with those nations. But within its own borders, black people were treated in a manner not greatly different from the treatment of Jews by the Nazis.* And a young black American was denied admission to aviation school because of the color of his skin; even the army, toward which he was vaguely drawn, offered little or no promise of advancement, because it too, as Bigger tells Max, is "Jim Crow" and "all they want a black man for is to dig ditches."

Equally striking in their treatment of the theme of social injustice are episodes related to the administration of justice. When Bigger and his three friends formulate their abortive plan to rob Blum's delicatessen, they know it will be the most difficult robbery they have ever attempted, for Blum is a white man. Before this, they had always robbed Negroes, feeling relatively safe in doing so, for "they knew that white policemen never really searched diligently for Negroes who committed crimes against other Negroes."

Nor does Bigger's trial for his admittedly heinous crimes exhibit any greater evidence of that impartiality which is the foundation of just legality. State's Attorney Buckley is permitted his sixty witnesses in spite of Max's argument that they are superfluous in the face of the defense's plea of guilty. And their testimony serves not only Buckley's avowed purpose of proving that Bigger is sane, proof the Attorney insists upon presenting in spite of Max's disavowal of insanity on his client's part, but the State's Attorney's undeclared intent of aggravating general feeling against Bigger, as when not one but six doctors testify that Bessie was raped. But Buckley does not rely on the words of his witnesses alone, but presents in climactic order every terrifying object pertaining to the murder, from the knife Bigger had hidden in a garbage pail to Mary's bones, the sight of which causes a woman in the courtroom to break into sobs. In a concluding display of histrionics, Buckley has the Dalton furnace brought in piece by piece and mounted upon a huge wooden platform. After directing a white girl, of Mary Dalton's size, to crawl into the furnace, so that spectators may see with their own eyes that Mary's body would fit into the space but that her head would not and thus had to be cut off, Buckley picks up an iron shovel and reenacts the discovery of the bones.

With such harrowing of emotions, and with a subsequent inflammatory speech, Buckley sets at naught Max's reasoned and logical appeal that Bigger's life be spared in reaffirmation of the basic American concepts of personal inviolability and the guarantee of its protection.

Thus, the *theme of social injustice and its dreadful consequences is developed in two ways*. First, the reader sees in Bigger himself, with his thwarted aspirations and his uncontrollable rages that lead inevitably to his hideous deeds, the end result of the deprivation of constitutionally guaranteed American rights. In the second place, the careful reader is brought to realize that true justice is not served by merely vindictive punishment; and that a just society, though carefully protecting itself against the depredations of the criminal, seeks not to destroy him, as he has destroyed others, but to restore him.

RACIAL CONFLICT. Closely related to the theme of social injustice, but by no means identical with it, is that of racial conflict. That theme is developed primarily in relation to Bigger himself, and it takes on varying appearances as the black native son's experiences are treated.

We first see Bigger's hostility toward a white society which has deprived him of opportunities for development as he engages in a street-corner conversation with his friend Gus on the morning of their planned robbery. There are references to white landlords who fail to provide their tenants with needed heat and to white boys who can fly because "they get a chance to do everything." To pass the time, the two young men "play white," a diversion described by Mr. Wright as "a game of play-acting in which [Bigger] and his friends imitated the ways and manners of white folks." As they act out absurd scenes in which Bigger portrays first a white general and then the President of the United States who commands his Secretary of State to interrupt his notes to Germany about "raising sand" in order to discuss the "niggers . . . raising sand all over the country," Bigger's tension mounts, and in spite of Gus's efforts to calm him, his resentment at his own deprived state finds expression in vehement words.

But the racial conflict presented in *Native Son* arises from efforts to help as well as from oppression. Mary Dalton's well-intentioned kindliness toward Bigger arouses his hatred, as he later admits to his lawyer Max. And his resentment of what seems to him to be patronizing condescension is extended, for a considerable time, to Jan, to a degree that Bigger deliberately implicates the young white man in his own crime.

Besides presenting racial conflict in terms of individual experience, the novel also treats it in mass situations. The wholesale harassment of the Negro community during the hunt for Bigger is graphically depicted, as is the behavior of white spectators at the time of his capture and during the inquest and the trial. Maniacal shouts of "Kill 'im!" "Lynch 'im" and "Black sonofabitch" resounded in Bigger's ears just before he loses consciousness as his flight ends. And when, after the inquest, Bigger is brought out of the Dalton home where he has refused to reenact his crime, he is confronted by the ultimate symbol of mindless white hatred, the flaming cross of the Ku Klux Klan.

The reader should bear in mind, however, that Richard Wright's presentation of racial conflict in all its ugliness and horror, is not a negation of hope for improvement. Although any reconciliation between black and white comes too late for Mary Dalton, for Bessie Mears, and for Bigger himself, the possibility and indeed the inevitability of such reconciliation is held forth. Even in Bigger's own case, although he pays the full penalty for his crimes, he comes before his execution to understand and to trust in two white men, his young Communist friend, Jan Erlone, and his aging Jewish lawyer, Boris A. Max.

Furthermore, Mr. Wright uses Max's words in Bigger's defense as an *eloquent plea for understanding between races and a shared effort toward creating an American society which will embody the principles articulated by the founders of the nation.* These words merit careful rereading by every student, for they will help him to comprehend the reasons for the racial conflict which is still manifest more than thirty years after the publication of *Native Son*, and to understand the necessity for reconciliation.

IDEOLOGY. When *Native Son* was published, Richard Wright had been a member of the Communist party for eight years. Although he made a final break with the party in 1944 because he felt it was no longer showing concern for the Negro cause, and although his own strong individualism had frequently led to strained relations, *Native Son* reflects his belief that the revolutionary aims of the party offered the Negro his best opportunity for meaningful participation in human history. The two most sympathetic white characters are both Communists, the young organizer, Jan Erlone, and the crusading lawyer, Boris A. Max. Furthermore, the most verbally anti-Communistic characters are as illogical and abusive in their attacks as any hysterical redbaiter today. Notable among such characters are Mr. Dalton's private investigator, Britten, and the State's Attorney, Buckley.

And yet in spite of the author's obvious belief that Communist ideology offers hope for black Americans, he is too honest and realistic to paint all those opposing it as bigots or opportunists. Peggy, the middle-aged Irish servant in the Dalton household, is genuinely concerned over her darling Mary's involvement with "reds" and cautions Bigger against being influenced by the girl's red friends, who, she avers, "just keep up a lot of fuss."

Nor is Bigger himself a convert to Communism. When Mary orders him to drive her to her rendezvous with Jan, he is beset with anxiety over having to meet a Communist with whom he wants no dealings. He would risk going to jail for robbery, but feels that "to go to jail for fooling around with reds was bunk." When Jan gives him Communist pamphlets, Bigger promises to read them but with no intent of keeping the promise, and after the murder he craftily plans to use them to incriminate Jan. And although he learns later to trust and respect both Jan and Max, there is no indication that he embraces their political philosophy. As he gropes toward awareness in the brief days between his sentence and his execution, he feels the need to question Max. But in their last talk together, only a few hours before Bigger goes to his death, the young black man's agonized questions are not directed toward schemes for world revolution, but toward the meaning of life itself.

VIOLENCE AS A PERSONAL NECESSITY. We come now to a theme of the novel most difficult to understand but also most pertinent to our immediate time. That is the concept of violence as a personal necessity. The student should be particularly on guard, as he considers this theme, against generalization. What Richard Wright was presenting in *Native Son* was an individual, a person whose circumstances made violence necessary for *him*. Regardless of the fact that our society has produced many Bigger Thomases (in this connection, the student is advised to look at Mr. Wright's "Introduction" to the book *Black Metropolis*); regardless of the fact that Bigger is therefore representational; he is at the same time the individualized protagonist of a particular literary work. *To understand Bigger fully is to understand those who, in our time, have lost all hope of changing intolerable conditions by peaceable method*, and have — in some cases deliberately; in others, without conscious volition — resorted to violence as a means of effecting their purposes. *It would be a mistake, however, to interpret this novel as advocating abandonment of non-violence.*

The student will remember that Bigger is characterized as a person subject to uncontrollable impulses, impulses stemming from fear and nurtured by hatred. Before the action of the novel began, these impulses, as we learn from Bigger's own statements to Max and from interior monologue, had resulted in minor infractions of the law and in commitment to a reformatory. In the first two books of *Native Son*, "Fear" and "Flight," we see the culmination of past experiences, both Bigger's own and that of his ancestors, in two brutal murders, of which the reader is not spared one horrifying detail. Both acts we come to see, were inevitable for Bigger — as was his death in the electric chair.

The necessity of such violence for Bigger is stated unequivocally in the last two pages of the novel. As Bigger appeals desperately to his white friend Max for answers to his questions, the latter tries to evade them, attempting to offer instead the comfort which the compassionate living feel they must extend to the dying. But Bigger pushes aside both the proffered comfort and the stale promises of better things for mankind as the result of political activity. And in spite of Max's terrified pleas to be spared the unbearable truth, Bigger forces it on him in these words:

> I didn't want to kill! . . . But what I killed for, I *am*! . . . What I killed for must've been good! . . . It must have been good! . . . I didn't know I was really alive in this world until I felt things hard enough to kill for 'em.

ACHIEVEMENT OF HUMAN FREEDOM. The theme we have just considered demands universal comprehension but does not imply universal applicability. However, this to which we now direct our attention, the achievement of human freedom, does. Freedom is a condition whose moral validity has been asserted by the great leaders of our civilization, both political and religious. *Native Son* discusses the achievement of human freedom on two levels, social and individual. We saw, when we examined plot structure, that *Richard Wright used a triadic pattern similar to the Hegelian dialectic, and that the three books of the novel, "Fear," "Flight," and "Fate," may be loosely compared to thesis, antithesis, and synthesis.* In the first two books the protagonist's deprivation of freedom, a deprivation which may be traced back to the enslavement of his forebears, leads to his destructive fears and his unsuccessful flight. In the third he is overtaken by fate, and condemned to be executed. So far, the novelistic treatment of freedom has been overwhelmingly negative; the reader is shown *what happens when freedom is destroyed.*

But the third book, "Fate," also presents a positive approach. In Boris A. Max's courtroom appeal for the life and rehabilitation of his young client, the presiding judge and all other listeners are reminded by the eloquent lawyer that freedom is promised by the American constitution, and that they have an opportunity to make the promise good. But because those who listen are still bound by their own fears and prejudices, both of which State's Attorney Buckley plays on cunningly, Max's efforts are futile and American society, as represented by that Chicago court, once again rejects the opportunity to free itself.

Paradoxically, however, *the individual, whose life that society is determined to snuff out, achieves his own freedom before his state-ordered extinction takes place.* What confers freedom upon Bigger is a developing awareness and a final willingness to face truth. Confronting the certainty of his own death, Bigger comes to an understanding of what makes life valuable. His resentment of his family's inadequacies changes to a comprehension of the cause, and compassion for the suffering; his sudden angers against his friends Gus, G. H., and Jack are transformed into a wish for better things for them; his fear and distrust of white people are replaced by respect and liking for Jan and Max; and finally, his wonder at what unfathomable mystery made people hate him so is transmuted into a knowledge that *even these people whose hatred had shaped his life were trying, like himself, to reach something beyond their grasp.*

The conclusive proof that Bigger has achieved his human freedom resides in one of his last statements to Max. Unlike the words most recently quoted, as terrifying to the reader as they are shown to be to the Jewish lawyer, these words evoke pity without terror.

> I'm all right, Mr. Max. Just go and tell Ma I was all right and not to worry none, see? Tell her I was all right and wasn't crying none.

COMMENT. As the student carefully rereads *Native Son* to discover its prevailing themes, he cannot fail to see how they are inextricably intertwined, as was pointed out previously. Thus the *five major themes* just examined — *social injustice, racial conflict, ideology, violence as a personal necessity*, and the *achievement of human freedom* — are each closely related and all are presented through the story of a young black American. But the student should never forget that for a novel to endure, its themes must transcend both time and place. If he reads thoughtfully, he comes to see that, although Richard Wright has utilized the experience he knows best and has not hesitated to particularize that experience to narrate what befell a young Negro living in the Chicago slums in the years just previous to this country's participating in World War II, the novelist has nonetheless presented *themes of universal significance*.

STYLISTIC QUALITIES

Because of emotional intensity and narrative power, *Native Son* tends to sweep the reader along by its own momentum. But the serious student, whatever the depths of his immersion in the story, should also be conscious of the author's stylistic skill. Mr. Wright's literary style in *Native Son* is noteworthy in two ways. *He has made use of effective contrasts in symbolic imagery*, and *he has varied the pattern of his prose to fit action or mood.*

CONTRASTS IN SYMBOLIC IMAGERY. By the time a student is ready for a serious novel like *Native Son*, he is likely to have been introduced, in both prose and poetry, to *symbol*, an object, character, or event which stands for something more than its surface meaning, and *imagery*, words and phrases which evoke from a reader one or more of the sensory responses — sight, sound, taste, touch, and smell. But as his artistic and literary sophistication increases, he will come to realize that symbol-hunting, the concentration on hidden meaning in everything encountered in a story, or a poem, can be self-defeating in that it may tend to obscure the total idea. For this reason we use the term *symbolic imagery* rather than *symbol* to designate Richard Wright's employment of images arising naturally from the setting and action he presents but at the same time conveying meanings greater than sensory representation. Such *symbolic imagery* can most profitably be studied in this novel as a series of contrasts.

The first of these contrasts, and certainly one which serves to deepen the reader's appreciation of theme, is the *contrast of black and white*. An obvious contrast in this category is, of course, the very coloring of characters. Nowhere is that difference of bodily appearance more strikingly illustrated than in the case of Bigger himself and the white person in whose presence he suffers his greatest unease, Mrs. Dalton. There are explicit references to

Bigger's blackness, as in the newspaper story he is allowed at the inquest, where his skin is described as "exceedingly black" and he is said to have a "dead-black complexion." And in contrast, at Bigger's first sight of Mrs. Dalton, we read, "Her face and hair were completely white, she seemed to him like a ghost."

But it is not Mrs. Dalton only who illustrates Bigger's fear of whiteness. When, on the occasion of Bigger's reluctant abetting Mary in flouting her parents' wishes, the Dalton heiress and her Communist friend insist on placing the young black man between them in the automobile, his reaction is presented by a metaphor which embodies similar color contrast: "he was sitting between two vast white looming walls."

Another striking black and white contrast involves the *organic image of the snow*, representing the menace which whiteness poses for Bigger, and the *black windows* of the empty buildings he passes in his desperate flight. Throughout the novel, snow is associated with Bigger's sense of dread, and nowhere is it more strongly conveyed than in the episode in which he conducts Bessie from her room to their last rendezvous. The two desperate young people go "into the snow, over the frozen streets, through the sweeping wind," and stop "in front of a tall, snow-covered building whose many windows gaped blackly, like the eye-sockets of empty skulls."

Less terrifying but equally effective in reminding the reader of the contrast between Bigger's black culture and the threatening white world is a *cinematic image*. While Bigger and Jack are waiting for the hour of their intended robbery, they decide to see a movie. They go to a double-feature. The first movie, "The Gay Woman," presents white men and women in a round of luxurious entertainment; the other, "Trader Horn," shows barbaric black people in an African jungle. Not only is the *black and white polarity* suggested here but the *merging of illusion and reality*. To Bigger and Jack the scenes showing white people on beaches or in night clubs are accurate depictions of a world as strange and remote as the African jungle.

The black and white contrasting symbolic imagery to be finally considered fully exemplifies the organic imagery which is an integral part of *naturalism, that literary method which is so named because it assumes that everything real exists in nature*. The student who reads such later novels by Richard Wright as *The Outsider* or *Savage Holiday* will be aware that the novelist did not remain completely in the naturalistic tradition established by earlier American novelists like Frank Norris, author of *McTeague*, or Theodore Dreiser, to whose *An American Tragedy* Mr. Wright's *Native Son* is often compared. But in the novel with which we are now concerned, he remained almost completely naturalistic. Thus the *animal imagery* constituting black and white contrast is especially appropriate.

The reader is introduced to the first of two *symbolic animals* on the second page of the novel, when a *huge black rat* invades the one-room apartment in which the four Thomases live. It must be destroyed to protect the family, and, with the aid of his younger brother, Bigger kills it with a blow from a heavy iron skillet. Before he takes successful aim, however, the animal runs "in a narrow circle, looking for a place to hide"; at one point it turns and rears upon its hind legs, its belly pulsing with fear and "its black beady eyes glittering." This episode serves as an adumbration of what will later happen to Bigger who is also regarded as a natural enemy and hunted down as mercilessly.

At still another point in the novel a black rat serves a symbolic purpose. Near the end of Book Two, "Flight," Bigger's self-preserving instinct has impelled him to search for an empty flat. Pausing near a street corner, he sees "a big black rat leaping over the snow." The reader should recognize further utilization here of the snow imagery previously mentioned, and the black rat's leaping over it will heighten his comprehension of Bigger's plight as the young black man frantically moves over a predominantly white world. In this instance, however, the fate of the black rat does not completely parallel Bigger's. As the human fugitive watches enviously, the animal darts to safety through a "gaping black hole."

As the black rat comes to stand for those menaced and ultimately destroyed by white society, so the rat's natural enemy becomes a symbol of the destructive force. On the occasion of Bigger's interview at the Dalton home, he sees a *huge white cat* pacing silently behind Mrs. Dalton, and the animal adds to his discomfiture by bounding to the table where Mr. Dalton has told him to lay his cap. After he has been installed in the most comfortable room of his life, he ventures to the kitchen for a drink of water, but is startled at finding Mrs. Dalton there with the cat, which fastens its eyes upon him. This incident foreshadows the part the cat will play in the impending cataclysm, for Bigger feels uneasy from looking at the woman and the white cat. Uneasiness develops into horror in the passage detailing Bigger's disposal of Mary's body. While he is frenziedly attempting to push the body far enough into the furnace to close the door, a noise makes him whirl. Perched on the trunk is the white cat, its eyes like "pools of accusation and guilt."

Once again on the next day, as reporters fill the basement, the cat is associated with Bigger's crime and his dread of discovery; after bounding down the steps it leaps upon Bigger's shoulder, clawing at his coat when he tries to put it down. The reporters take pictures, one of which he sees in a paper he buys just before returning to Bessie's room to conduct her to her death. Describing the newspaper picture, the author emphasizes the black-white contrast, by explicit use of the two adjectives applicable respectively to man and animal, and underscores the ominous symbolism by repeating the metaphorical reference to the cat's eyes as "twin pools of secret guilt." The student should note here how *a double significance becomes attached to the black-white contrast.* Although to Bigger the white cat's eyes convey an accusation of his own guilt, that which is seen in their depths may just as well refer to the guilt borne by white civilization.

Besides black and white imagery, a second kind of contrast is provided in *metallic symbols*. Bigger is not only the product of a historical process set in motion when the first black captive was brought to American shores, he is also the victim of a harshly mechanized society, where human tenderness is powerless against the hardness of metal structures. Throughout the novel metallic imagery is used to convey rigidity and painful hardness, as when Bigger tells his friend Gus that thinking of white people's treatment of him makes him feel that a "red-hot iron" is being thrust down his throat. However, the most memorable instances of the powerful effect of metallic objects and metallic sound upon Bigger's life occur respectively at the beginning of Book One and the conclusion of Book Three. The novel opens with an *onomatopoetic reproduction* of the clang of an alarm clock, thus: Brrrrrrriiiiiiiiii-iiiiinng! Bigger's mother calls to him to turn it off. So Bigger is not only deprived abruptly of the "balm of hurt minds," as Shakespeare's Macbeth called sleep, but he must also shuffle in his naked feet across a wooden floor in order to bring the disturbing sound to an end.

In contrast to the harsh interruption of Bigger's sleep which, for all of its disruptive effect, announces the beginning of a new day, is the finality of the closing doors on the last page of Book Three — and of the novel itself. These are Mr. Wright's words: "He heard the ring of steel against steel as a far door clanged shut." To fully appreciate the stylistic skill reflected in these two instances of metallic imagery, the student should note that Richard Wright has used the same verb, *clanged*, to convey the sound of the steel doors closing as he used in the passage concerning the alarm clock. Like the artificial word with which Book One opens, *clang* is an *onomatopoetic word*, that is, *a word which sounds like what it represents*. Thus *the story of Bigger Thomas begins with an auditory assault upon the nervous system and ends with it*. At no point in his brief life has Bigger been free from dissonance, nor is he spared its pain as his life nears its close.

The third kind of contrasting imagery used by Mr. Wright is *totemic, pertaining to a venerated emblem,* in this case the cross. When Bigger is visited by the Reverend Hammond, the pastor of his mother's church, at the Cook County Morgue where the coroner's inquest is held, the black minister puts around the young man's neck a chain upon which is a small wooden cross.

Because the preacher's words have aroused in Bigger a response to the Christian story which he has heard all his life, he makes no resistance, but wears the cross next to his skin all during the agonizing inquest and again when he is taken afterward to the Dalton home in an effort to force him into a reenactment of his crime. As he emerges from the house, surrounded by police, he is reviled and spat upon by a vicious mob. Stumbling along, he becomes aware of a "high bright object" and looks up. He sees on top of a building a flaming cross. Before he realizes what it signifies, he recalls the preacher's having said to him that the lowly Jesus had carried a cross for everyone. Momentarily, Bigger wonders whether the cross on the building means that white people want him to love Jesus too. But he also feels that it is not right to burn a cross, and then full understanding comes. ". . . that cross was not the cross of Christ but the cross of the Ku Klux Klan. He had a cross of salvation around his throat and they were burning one to tell him that they hated him."

By thus juxtaposing the two *contrasting totemic images*, the small wooden cross on a chain and the large flaming cross on a building, *Richard Wright has clearly represented the distinction between the claim of our nation to be a Christian one and the actions which flagrantly belie that claim.* We have already noted how Bigger vehemently rejects the Christian religion after this demonstration, by throwing his cross away and repeatedly refusing efforts to restore it to him. Thus the imagery of the two crosses represents the inefficacy of a religion whose principles are not practiced by those who profess to believe in them.

VARIATION IN PROSE. Besides the stylistic devices we have just considered, Richard Wright utilizes a variety of sentence patterns, each one adapted to the event or situation presented.

In the first place, action which involves little or no reflection is generally presented in brief sentences, interspersed now and then with slightly longer ones. Two examples will suffice to demonstrate stylistic effectiveness. The first, found in Book One, narrates Bigger's brutal treatment of his friend Gus in Doc's poolroom, treatment stemming from Bigger's own fear.

> Gus looked round the room without moving his head, just rolling his eyes in a mute appeal for help. But no one moved. Bigger's left fist was slowly lifting to strike. Gus's lips moved toward the knife; he stuck out his tongue and touched the blade. Gus's lips quivered and tears streamed down his cheeks ... Bigger watched Gus with lips twisted in a crooked smile.

All but one of the seven sentences is simple, and that one is compound, its two principal clauses written in regular order: subject-verb-and-modifier or complement. And the shortest sentence contains only four words.

The second example occurs in Book Two, near the end of Bigger's flight, as he lies on the top of a water tank.

> He did not move; he lay with gun in hand, waiting. Then, directly under his eyes, four white fingers caught hold of the icy edge of the water tank. He gritted his teeth and struck the white fingers with the butt of the gun. They vanished and he heard a thud as a body landed on the snow-covered roof.

Although sentences in this passage are generally longer than in the first, such length increases the reader's feeling of suspense and terror, only momentarily relieved as Bigger strikes the white fingers.

The narrative passages of *Native Son* demonstrate not only Mr. Wright's mastery of prose, but also of dialogue. The student has already had his attention drawn to the author's facility in reproducing human speech, so that it should not be necessary here to furnish additional illustration. He should recall, however, that *dialogue is often terse and monosyllabic*, as in the conversation among Jan, Mary, and Bigger in Ernie's Kitchen Shack. And even in the presence of persons with whom Bigger is more at ease than with his white companions, *speech is couched in short phrases*. A striking occurrence of limited verbal communication between two people who have experienced physical intimacy is found in passages involving Bigger and Bessie. When the young man visits the black girl after his second interrogation by Britten and his men, their conversation assumes the following pattern:

> "Bigger?"
> He turned and looked at her.
> "What?"
> "You ain't really planning to do that, sure 'nough?"
> "What the hell you think?"
> "Bigger, naw!"

By careful rereading, the student will be able to find repeated examples of the above. He should occasionally read aloud, for by so doing he will more fully appreciate Mr. Wright's mastery of his characters' speech. Whether the reader has ever actually heard persons whose formal education is limited, he will know from the very sound of the words that this reproduction is right and true.

Another instance of the novelist's *varying his prose to fit the occasion* is seen in his use of *Biblical rhythms*. The King James version of the Old and New Testaments has shaped the style of most major American authors, and Richard Wright is no exception. Furthermore, this black writer is well aware that Americans who rarely put pen to paper tend to think in the English of the King James Bible, because they have heard it so often from their ministers. Thus, the passage describing Bigger's reaction to the Reverend Hammond's recapitulation of Creation and Redemption echoes the very words of the first chapter of Genesis, intermingling them with a rhythmic evocation of the young black man's emotions.

> . . . there emerged slowly a huge shining ball and the voice said *let there be light* and there was light and it was good light and the voice said *let there be a firmament* and the waters parted . . .

Similar to such expression of Bigger's meditation in its use of prolonged sentences uninterrupted by ordinary punctuation, but differing in word choice, is the kind of prose used for Bigger's love-making. Although the novelist is at pains to show that the circumstances of Bigger's and Bessie's lives prevent their ever developing the tenderness and self-forgetfulness which are essential in genuine love, he demonstrates, nonetheless, that their brief physical union transcends both their character defects and the squalor of their surroundings.

> . . . he floated on a wild tide, rising and sinking with the ebb and flow of her blood . . ., clinging close to a fountain whose warm waters washed and cleansed his senses . . .

COMMENT. From the foregoing discussion and brief excerpts, the student should be better prepared to understand and analyze the stylistic features of *Native Son*. Foremost among them is Mr. Wright's consistently effective use of *contrasts in symbolic imagery*, particularly the pervasive black-white contrast. The attentive reader will discover a great many more of these contrasts than those specifically cited here. He may also find multiple examples of *contrasting auditory imagery*, and of *contrasting totemic symbols*, that is, symbols associated with cultural religion. In addition, his own awareness of the uses to which prose may be put will be deepened. He will see how Mr. Wright's *short simple sentences speed up violent action*, and how *longer sentences with modifying phrases help to intensify suspense*. Speech will become very real for him through terse and prevailingly monosyllabic dialogue. Finally, he will be made to realize how prose itself can be made poetic as he notes examples of *stream-of-consciousness*, both those containing Biblical language and those conveying emotional release.

SURVEY OF CRITICISM OF *NATIVE SON*

From the time of its publication in 1940 until the present, *Native Son* has elicited a variety of critical responses, some of which are almost wholly pejorative. To the latter Mr. Wright himself replied on more than one occasion, and some additional literary arguments have arisen because of differing assessments of the novel. Most valuable to the student are analyses of *Native Son* which take into account both its merits and defects — although there is a lack of agreement as to what constitutes either — and which attempt to establish its position as an American novel.

WRIGHT'S OWN COMMENTARY. What a writer himself has to say about his method and his purpose can be illuminating. On June 1, 1940, an article by Wright entitled "How Bigger Was Born" appeared in the *Saturday Review*. In this article Mr. Wright told of five "Biggers" he had known in the South, beginning with a child who bullied his playmates, and including slightly older Negroes who resorted to violence in their revolt against Southern "Jim Crow" laws. Each of the five met an untimely death, according to either Mr. Wright's certain knowledge or his logical supposition. When he moved to Chicago, he saw other "Biggers," and gradually came to the realization that there were white "Biggers" also, young men irremediably conditioned toward crime. Mr. Wright attributes this discovery to his own association with the labor movement and also to his reading. As he was increasingly impelled to put his developing knowledge of "Bigger" into a book, he was beset by fears that he would be misunderstood, but he eventually realized that he must present his protagonist with complete honesty, withholding nothing of the wretchedness of his existence or the horror of his crimes.

Besides affording information on the source of the novel, Mr. Wright's article offers proof of the painstaking artistry we observed in our examination of structure and style. He finished the first draft, he tells us, in four months of daily work. But he was not satisfied with that first draft, and reworked the book, developing themes he had only hinted at and revising the conclusion. The final paragraph of his article pays tribute to earlier American writers, Hawthorne and James, and to the great master of horror, Poe.

REVIEWS AND CRITICAL STUDIES. Immediately upon publication of *Native Son*, the novel was widely reviewed by the best-known reviewers of the time. Contributing to its widespread fame was the fact that it was selected by the Book-of-the-Month Club, the company which has for many years sold books by subscription, choice of titles being made by an editorial board composed of literary experts. For that organization's newsletter, Henry Seidel Canby wrote of the novel's engrossing story and its power to arouse sympathy for the Negro. Dorothy Canfield Fisher, herself a widely read novelist, writing the Introduction to the first edition, compared the handling of subject matter to that of Dostoevsky, the Russian author of such masterpieces as *Crime and Punishment* and *The Brothers Karamazov*. But a more frequent comparison was made to the American novelist, John Steinbeck. Writing for the *New Yorker*, Clifton Fadiman spoke of *Native Son* as the most powerful American novel since Steinbeck's *The Grapes of Wrath*; Samuel Sillen claimed, in an article in *New Masses*, that Wright's novel like Steinbeck's would move readers to a new conception of reality; Margaret Marshall, in the *Nation*, found a maturity of thought and feeling surpassing that of *The Grapes of Wrath*; and Malcolm Cowley, writing in the *New Republic*, pointed out specific resemblances between the two novels, such as their treatment of the dispossessed and their relation to the radical movement of the preceding decade.

In both contemporary reviews, however, and later critical studies, another comparison occurs more frequently, that between Mr. Wright's novel and Theodore Dreiser's *An American Tragedy*, first published in 1925. Early reviewers who pointed out the parallels between these stories of young men forced into criminality by society and then executed were Charles Poore, in the *New York Times* and Edward Skillen, Jr., in *Commonweal*; Clifton Fadiman, whose comparison to Steinbeck's work we have already noted, also places *Native Son* in the same category as *An American Tragedy*, even though considering Dreiser's work the greater.

Among later critical studies, Charles I. Glicksberg's "Negro Fiction in America," which appeared first in the *South Atlantic Quarterly* for October 1946, found some features of Wright's characterization of Bigger displaying the same kind of realism as Dreiser's, that is, the effect of environment on human development. To Glicksberg, however, Bigger's becoming a killer went beyond realism into propaganda. One year later, in *The Novel and the World's Dilemma*, Edwin Berry Burgum asserted that Mr. Wright had followed the general plan of *An American Tragedy* up until the trial scene. At that point, according to Burgum, Richard Wright abandoning Dreiser's method, substituted the symbolic for the objective. It was, said this critic, an unsuccessful change in method, because it offered no hope. Heretofore, stated Burgum, Wright had been able, like Dreiser, to stand apart from his character's deeds, but in the trial scene, and in Bigger's final belief that murder had freed him from oppression, the author became identified with the social malady he was describing.

Even among contemporary reviews, reaction to *Native Son* was not totally favorable. Writing in the *Atlantic Monthly* for May 1940, David L. Cohn called the novel a "study in hate," and accused Richard Wright of not sticking to facts, asserting that Negroes had political rights in all states outside the South. He equated Richard Wright's attitude toward whites with that of the Ku Klux Klan toward Negroes, and contrasted the novelist's insistence upon civil rights for black people as an immediate solution with the patience of Jews in England who waited five centuries for their political equality.

Richard Wright was quick to reply. In June the *Atlantic Monthly* published his "I Bite the Hand that Feeds Me." With occasional acrimonious references to the distinction between Negroes and

Jews, the novelist refuted the charge that his work exhibited hatred of whites, and made a justifiable *distinction between defending a crime and explaining what caused an individual to commit it*. And he exhibited considerable satisfaction in correcting a factual error. Mr. Cohn had asserted incorrectly that Bigger's age was not stated in the novel; Mr. Wright cited two statements, one by Bigger himself, the other in the judge's words upon sentencing the young man, and gave page numbers for each instance.

In the same month that David L. Cohn's article appeared in the *Atlantic Monthly*, Burton Rascoe attacked *Native Son* in the *American Mercury*, calling it one of the worst novels, in spite of technical excellence, he had ever read, and charging it with three serious faults: substitution of authorial comment for development of moral through action and speech, allowing Bigger awareness of the forces that impelled him to crime, and inconsistency in characterization of Bigger. Once again, Richard Wright was allowed to reply in the same magazine, and he did so with fine indignation, declaring that Mr. Rascoe's reaction proved the validity of Max's courtroom statement that men made to feel guilty of wrong will attempt to justify themselves.

BALDWIN AND ELLISON. Controversy concerning the merits and defects of *Native Son* was not confined to the year of its publication. One of the most interesting critical developments arose from assessments made by the younger black novelist whose fame has equaled or even exceeded Wright's, James Baldwin. For complete understanding of Mr. Baldwin's attitude toward the older writer, both as artist and person, the student should read "Alas, Poor Richard" in the collection of essays entitled *Nobody Knows My Name*. But since that essay is concerned with other writings and with Baldwin's personal memories of the man sixteen years older than himself who had been his idol, we need only note here that he pays tribute to *Native Son* as being one of the first works in which he found expressed all the bitterness and anger he too had felt. In an earlier essay, however, "Many Thousands Gone," Baldwin points out what to him are the faults of *Native Son*. In Baldwin's opinion, Richard Wright did not succeed in making a person of Bigger, but only a social symbol. Furthermore, Max's long speech at the trial, Baldwin says, fails to clarify Bigger's humanity, for Wright had shown the young Negro as a monster created by American society.

Irving Howe, in "Black Boys and Native Sons," countered Baldwin's criticism with an assertion that Richard Wright's purpose was to show the violence which is part of the American Negro's life and which mars him in a way no other American is marred. And he claimed that younger novelists like Baldwin and Ralph Ellison had been able to move away from naturalism only because Wright had written so courageously.

Quick to respond to Irving Howe's assertion was Mr. Ellison, whom the student probably knows best through *Invisible Man*, but who is the author also of much excellent shorter writing, both fiction and criticism. In the essay "The World and the Jug," Ralph Ellison disclaimed Richard Wright as his "spiritual father," explaining that, on the contrary, Wright was simply a good friend in whose magazine Mr. Ellison's first book review was published. Paying tribute to the older novelist's accomplishment in *Native Son*, Ellison nonetheless insisted that Bigger Thomas is not the ultimate representative of the American Negro.

One other subjective reaction to James Baldwin's evaluation should be noted, that of Eldridge Cleaver, the black militant whose provocative book *Soul on Ice* was written during his incarceration in Folsom Prison. In the chapter which uses as its title a slight variation of Baldwin's "Notes of a Native Son," substituting *on* for *of*, Mr. Cleaver attacked what he considered Baldwin's repudiation of Richard Wright's masculinity. To Cleaver, Baldwin's statement in "Alas, Poor Richard" that Richard Wright's social, political, and historical ideas did not correspond to reality simply reveals Baldwin's own inadequacies. Far from being politically confused, Richard Wright displays, according to Mr. Cleaver, a profundity in his dealing with politics, the economy, and American society. And Mr. Cleaver lauds the characterization of Bigger Thomas. He is to him as to the majority of critics, Wright's "greatest creation," contrasting that characterization with Rufus Scott, a character in Baldwin's *Another Country*. To Cleaver, Bigger Thomas's violent rebellion against white society is infinitely superior to Scott's submission to it.

THEMATIC AND FORMALISTIC ANALYSES. In the foregoing brief summary of Eldridge Cleaver's angry rejection of James Baldwin's criticism, the word *subjective* was used. The student should remember that all writing is, to a degree, subjective, for no one writes in a vacuum, and a certain amount of personal feeling enters into any kind of critical analysis. Nevertheless, he should learn to distinguish between criticism obviously colored by irrelevant or peripheral issues and criticism applying accepted literary criteria in a structured analysis of any piece of writing. Of the latter nature are the two articles we shall finally consider.

A valuable source for any study of the American novel, particularly as it has been produced by black writers, is Robert A. Bone's *The Negro Novel in America*. In that work, first published in 1958 and revised in 1965, Mr. Bone carefully analyzes *Native Son* as a "protest" novel. Relating Richard Wright's own experience to the creation of Bigger, this critic finds of particular significance Mr. Wright's membership in the Communist party and his eventual break with it. Bigger's relationship with Jan and Max, Mr. Bone feels, can be explained by the conflict Wright felt as a Negro nationalist attempting to relate to white Party members. And the critic also thinks that one defect in *Native Son* stems from the novelist's inability to keep the great thematic conflicts between love and hate and between Negro solidarity and general human brotherhood within the chief character. In Mr. Bone's view, the utilization of Jan and Max as mouthpieces for an ideal weakens the novel. However, he considers that, of Negro novelists writing between 1930 and 1940, Richard Wright most nearly expressed the spirit of the time. Thus, Wright's contribution to the Negro novel was his union of racial pride and social protest.

Falling more within the area of formalistic criticism, that is, the kind of criticism which analyzes a writer's use of form in the presentation of his theme, is a study by James A. Emanuel, "Fever and Feeling: Notes on the Imagery in *Native Son*," which was first published in *Negro Digest* for December 1968. Professor Emanuel believes that Richard Wright's imagery in *Native Son* conveys the very fabric of consciousness in a method comparable to that of the great American novelist, Henry James. We have already noted Wright's use of contrasting symbolic images. In addition to those which we took account of, Professor Emanuel's essay cites contrasts of light and dark, and stresses the importance of the furnace in the basement. He also calls attention to a repeated image of Bigger's — his seeking the center of whatever room he may be in — an image which reminds the critic of a similar use by Chekhov. As employed by Mr. Wright, according to Professor Emanuel, the image demonstrates how badly Bigger is constricted and how sorely he needs a liberating sense of space.

Another recurring image cited by this critic is that of "blotting out." This reveals Bigger's impulse to destroy that which circumvents his own fulfillment, but it is used in reverse when white society wishes to erase Bigger's very life.

Professor Emanuel also finds effective such images as that of a wall or a curtain, used first to show how Bigger is separated from white society. Later in the novel, says the critic, as Bigger acquires a new perceptiveness, he longs fervently to have the walls torn down.

Professor Emanuel concludes his essay by reminding readers that a recognition of Mr. Wright's images does not guarantee a complete understanding of Bigger. Nevertheless, the reader has an obligation to understand Bigger as a human being. And, he says, Mr. Wright's images have dramatized the black man's condition in America, which the reader, having been aroused by the imagery, can begin to comprehend.

> COMMENT. The foregoing survey of critical opinion on *Native Son* from 1940 through the 1960's reveals a wide variety of response to *Native Son*, including some almost

completely unfavorable assessments. And among those who acclaim the novel, there is frequently disagreement concerning the effectiveness of certain passages, such as Max's courtroom speech. Too, there is a range of comparison with other authors, both American and foreign, from Dreiser and Steinbeck, to Dostoevsky and Chekhov. Nor is this summary in any way exhaustive. The student should constantly attempt to increase his own interpretive powers by thoughtful reading of both the critics mentioned above and others he will find cited in the Bibliography to this Study Guide. He should also be on the lookout for even later analyses, since interest in *Native Son* continues to grow and new interpretations are constantly appearing.

ESSAY QUESTIONS AND ANSWERS

1. Discuss the structural framework of *Native Son*.

ANSWER. In place of the usual division into chapters found in most novels, *Native Son* has three major divisions or books, titled respectively "Fear," "Flight," and "Fate." Such a triadic structure is reminiscent of the Hegelian dialectic of thesis, antithesis, and synthesis, in which an existing force or entity gives rise to its own opposite, and the conflict between the two is resolved by the formation of a new entity or force. It is a structural pattern peculiarly appropriate for a novel dealing with a young black American's experience in the late 1930's, when many an intellectual, including Wright himself, looked for solution of the problems besetting the nation to Karl Marx's dialectical materialism, itself an adaptation of the Hegelian dialectic. It is out of the fear surrounding the existence of the protagonist, Bigger Thomas, that flight arises, but neither fear nor flight suffices, and the only resolution is in Bigger's acceptance of his fate. Contributing further to the effectiveness of such structure, is the pace it imparts to the movement of the novel. Without the pauses unavoidably occasioned by chapter divisions, the reader moves swiftly and breathlessly with Bigger from the moment he awakens to the metallic clangor of an alarm clock on a Saturday morning, through the events which culminate in his murder of his white employer's daughter, Mary Dalton, and his fleeing with his girl, Bessie, whom he also murders, to his capture. And though the third book, "Fate," comprises a slightly longer time period, it too is tightly packed with both external events and Bigger's internal struggle, up to the very day of his execution. The only prolonged portion is the trial itself, where the speeches of Boris Max, who defends Bigger, and the State's Attorney, Buckley, cover more than twenty pages. However, both those speeches are essential to a complete understanding not only of Bigger's fate, but that of the nation which produced him.

2. How effective is character development in *Native Son*?

ANSWER. The only fully developed character in the novel is Bigger himself. Every means available to a novelist is utilized to present this young black man whose horrid crimes arouse terror and revulsion, but whose individual suffering evokes pity and compassion. The reader knows his age, twenty; his appearance, with very black skin, and a lithe, muscular body, which assumes an awkward hulking posture in the presence of white people; his speech, generally brief and monosyllabic; his uncontrollable rages; his vague yearnings toward a better life; his sense of frustration and bitterness; and finally his dawning understanding of himself and other men, an understanding which enables him on the eve of his electrocution to send a message to his mother that he is "all right" and not crying.

Although no other person in the novel is so completely developed as Bigger, the black characters are sketched with incisive strokes, so that the reader sees and knows the rest of the Thomas family: Bigger's pious, hard-working mother; his timid, skinny adolescent sister, Vera; and his aggressively loyal little brother, Buddy. Also individualized are his girl, Bessie, who finds escape from drudgery only through drink and Bigger's love-making; his three friends, Jack, G. H., and Gus; and the devout pastor of his mother's church, the Reverend Hammond. The white characters are not so believably delineated, largely because Bigger himself cannot understand them; but Mr. Wright gives us enough descriptive detail for visualization: Mr. Dalton, tall, lean, and white-haired, a philanthropist who provides ping-pong tables for Negro youth but charges his Negro tenants exorbitant rents for slum dwellings; Mrs. Dalton, also tall, thin, and white-haired, her sightless eyes serving symbolically to denote a corresponding blindness to human needs; Mary, their daughter, pretty, slender, dark-haired, in rebellion against her parents' conventionality but no more knowledgeable than they concerning the real life of Bigger and others like him; Jan Erlone, Mary's idealistic young Communist friend, blond, handsome, kindly. Besides these whites, there are some unsympathetic characterizations, particularly of Britten, Mr.

Dalton's private investigator, whose treatment of both Bigger and Jan reveals his own bullying and imperceptive nature, and Buckley, the State's Attorney, who deliberately plays on the fears and prejudices of his white hearers in order to convict Bigger and thereby advance his own political position. The most important white character, however, is Boris A. Max, the Jewish lawyer who defends Bigger so fervently and so eloquently, but who cannot, at the last, bear to face the extent of Bigger's commitment to death.

3. Comment on major themes in *Native Son*.

ANSWER. Since the very title of the novel suggests the irony of America's treatment of a person born on her soil, one of its major themes is social injustice. This theme is made explicit in Max's long courtroom speech, tracing the history of this nation's treatment of the Negro, from his being wrested brutally from his first home and brought to these shores in bondage, through an Emancipation which freed him technically but not actually, to the economic deprivations he continues to suffer in a land whose scientific and industrial progress are the envy of the world. But the theme is more immediately conveyed through the accounts of Bigger's squalid living conditions, especially in the episode involving the rat; of the frustration felt by his companions and himself at their being limited to the most menial jobs and the impossibility of their learning to fly a plane; and of Bigger's instinctive feeling that he must affect a humble obsequiousness in the presence of whites.

Closely associated with the theme of social injustice is that of racial conflict. To Bigger the white world is an alien world, and a portion of the horror he experiences at his unplanned murder of Mary is alleviated by a sense of exultation that he, who is considered stupid and insignificant by white people, has actually killed one of them and outwitted them in their attempts to discover the identity of the killer. Equally illustrative of racial conflict is the mass hysteria exhibited by white Chicagoans during the pursuit of Bigger, with wholesale dismissal of Negro employees and the invasion of Negro homes and the violence inflicted upon any who attempt to resist. The reference to the white mob's violence brings to mind a third theme, perhaps the most difficult to accept, that of violence as a personal necessity. Though the novel does not attempt to extenuate the crime of murder, it does show that only through that crime did Bigger achieve realization. He himself tells a vainly protesting Max that although he did not want to kill, what he killed for must have been good. Related to that theme, but less painful to come to grips with, is the achievement of human freedom. The novel makes clear that all Americans must be freed from want and fear, but it also makes clear an equal necessity in the achievement of both general and individual freedom, the abolition of hate and its replacement by love. Bigger gradually ceases to hate even those who show hatred to him, for he sees, however dimly, that they too wanted something they did not have. And for those who have tried to help him, both his bewildered family and his articulate white friends, Jan and Max, his last spoken words are messages of reassurance and comfort.

4. What are the distinguishing stylistic qualities of *Native Son*?

ANSWER. One of the most effective stylistic devices in *Native Son* is a series of contrasting symbolic images. There is a notable black-white contrast, which serves to represent both Bigger's alienation from the dominant white society and that society's rejection of him. Illustrative of this particular imagery are such contrasts as Bigger's skin tone and Mrs. Dalton's white skin and hair, the black pavement of the city streets and the falling white snow, the motion picture *Trader Horn* depicting African life and the other part of the twin bill, *The Gay Woman*, featuring the luxurious life of white high society, and, most striking of all, the two animal symbols, the white cat who seems to Bigger both witness and accuser, and the black rat whose frantic efforts at escape and whose final destruction adumbrate Bigger's own fate. Another pair of contrasting images is the clanging of the alarm clock which awakens Bigger on the February morning when we first encounter him and the clanging of steel on steel as the prison door closes behind him for the last time. Finally, there is a contrast symbolizing both Bigger's tentative acceptance of religious consolation and his ultimate rejection of it in the wooden cross placed on him by the Reverend Hammond and the burning cross atop a building after the inquest. The sight of the latter impels him to fling away the small cross, vehemently and repeatedly. Another notable stylistic device is the variation in prose according to the mood or purpose of the passage: brief sentences for ordinary action or swiftly moving events; terse, monosyllabic dialogue; Biblical rhythm in Bigger's meditations; stream-of-consciousness as love-making brings temporary release or, later, as Bigger tries to fathom the meaning of existence.

5. To what extent does the novel stress a particular ideology?

ANSWER. At the time Richard Wright was composing *Native Son*, he had not made his break with the Communist party. Consequently, it is not surprising that the two most sympathetic characters, Jan Erlone and Boris A. Max, are Communists. Furthermore, Max's long speech at the trial and his private conversations with Bigger suggest that only Communism can solve the problem of Bigger and others like him. But in spite of Wright's own political affiliation, he was too much the conscientious artist to force his protagonist into a mold. Bigger knows little of Communism at the beginning of the novel and is shocked to learn that Mary Dalton has Communist friends. He resents Jan's giving him Party literature, and is puzzled by Britten's attempts to trap him into admission of Party membership. When he tries to extort money from Mr. Dalton, he signs the false kidnap note "Red," and draws below it the Communist emblem of the hammer and sickle, remembering what he had seen on the pamphlets but thinking of the sickle only as a round kind of knife with a handle. And even in the enlightenment which comes to him in the days before his execution, he finds no answer to his questions in Communism, in spite of his growing love for Jan and Max. Thus, the novel is not primarily ideological; it transcends political theories in its exploration of the mind and heart of Bigger Thomas.

6. Discuss the place of *Native Son* in the American literary tradition.

ANSWER. In some respects, *Native Son* is the culmination of American naturalism, the literary school which shows man at the mercy of forces over which he can exercise no control. The other American novel to which *Native Son* is most frequently compared is Theodore Dreiser's *An American Tragedy*. Dreiser's white protagonist, Clyde Griffiths, yearned, like Bigger, for the things his society had taught him to desire, but for the attainment of which he had been given no provision. Like Bigger, Clyde murdered and was executed, helpless either to control his impulses or avert his fate. But Mr. Wright's novel belongs to still another category, that of the protest novel. The conditions which produce Bigger and force him into crime are those to which American Negroes have been subjected throughout their history, and it is against those conditions that the novel cries out in protest. For the present there is a third classification into which *Native Son* fits, the obvious category of the Negro novel. But it seems likely that even when those three terms, *naturalistic, protest, Negro*, no longer seem as significant as now, *Native Son* will retain its place among great American novels as a book which records a vital part of the total American experience.

BIBLIOGRAPHY

For the most complete listing of Richard Wright's own works the student should consult "Richard Wright (1908-1960)," by Michel Fabré and Edward Margolies, which appeared first in the *Bulletin of Bibliography*, XXIV (1965), 131-133, 137, and was reprinted in Constance Webb, *Richard Wright, A Biography*, New York: G. P. Putnam's Sons, 1968, pp. 423-429. He should note also that some of the works listed here include valuable bibliographies, particularly Richard Wright's *Native Son: A Critical Handbook*, edited by Richard Abcarian, and *Dark Symphony*, edited by James A. Emanuel and Theodore L. Gross. Abcarian's *Handbook* reprints many valuable critiques.

WORKS BY RICHARD WRIGHT

Uncle Tom's Children: Four Nouvellas. New York: Harper & Bros., 1938.

Native Son. New York: Harper & Bros., 1940.

———, *with Afterword by John Reilly.* (A Perennial Classic) New York: Harper & Row, Publishers, 1966.

"How Bigger Was Born." *Saturday Review*, XXII (June 1, 1940), 17-20.

"I Bite the Hand That Feeds Me." *Atlantic Monthly*, CLXV (June 1940), 826-828.

Black Boy; a Record of Childhood and Youth. New York: Harper and Bros., 1945.

————————————————. (A perennial Classic) New York: Harper & Row, Publishers, 1966.

Eight Men. Cleveland and New York: Avon, 1961.

———. New York: Pyramid Books, 1969.

CRITICAL AND BIOGRAPHICAL WORKS

ABCARIAN, RICHARD, ed. *Richard Wright's Native Son: A Critical Handbook*. Belmont, California: Wadsworth Publishing Company, Inc., 1970.

BALDWIN, JAMES. "Many Thousands Gone." *Notes of a Native Son*. Boston: Beacon Press, 1955, pp. 24-26.

─── "Alas, Poor Richard." *Nobody Knows My Name*. New York: The Dial Press, 1961, pp. 181-215.

BONE, ROBERT A. "Native Son: A Novel of Social Protest." *The Negro Novel in America*. Revised ed. New Haven: Yale University Press, 1965, pp. 142-152.

BURGUM, EDWIN BERRY. "The Promise of Democracy in Richard Wright's *Native Son*." *The Novel and the World's Dilemma*. New York: Oxford University Press, 1947.

CANBY, HENRY SEIDEL. Review. *Book-of-the-Month-Club News* (February 1940), pp. 2-3.

CLEAVER, ELDRIDGE. "Notes On a Native Son." *Soul on Ice*. New York: Dell Publishing Co., 1968, pp. 97-111.

COHN, DAVID L. Review. *Atlantic Monthly*, CLXV (May 1940), 656-661.

COWLEY, MALCOLM. Review. *New Republic* (March 18, 1940).

ELLISON, RALPH W. "Richard Wright's Blues." *Black Expression*, ed. by Addison Gayle, Jr. New York: Weybright and Talley, 1969, pp. 311-325.

───. "The World and the Jug." *Shadow and Act*. New York: Random House, 1964.

EMANUEL, JAMES A. "Fever and Feeling: Notes on the Imagery in Native Son." *Negro Digest*, XVIII (December 1968), 16-26.

─── and THEODORE L. GROSS, eds. "Richard Wright, 1908-1960." *Dark Symphony: Negro Literature in America*. New York: The Free Press, 1968, pp. 222-226.

FADIMAN, CLIFTON. Review. *The New Yorker*, XVI (March 2, 1940), 52-53.

GLICKSBERG, CHARLES I. "Negro Fiction in America." *South Atlantic Quarterly*, XLV (October 1946), 478-488.

HOWE, IRVING. "Black Boys and Native Sons." *A World More Attractive*. New York: Horizon Press, 1963, pp. 98-110.

MARGOLIES, EDWARD. "Richard Wright: *Native Son* and Three Kinds of Revolution." *Native Sons: A Critical Study of Twentieth-Century Negro American Authors.* New York: J. B. Lippincott Company, 1968, pp. 65-86.

MARSHALL, MARGARET. Review. *Nation*, CL (March 16, 1940), 367-368.

RASCOE, BURTON. Review. *American Mercury*, L (May 1940), 113-116.

SCOTT, NATHAN A., JR. "Search for Beliefs: The Fiction of Richard Wright." *University of Kansas City Review*, XXIII (1956), 19-24.

SILLEN, SAMUEL. Review. *New Masses*, XXXIV (March 5, 1940), 24-25.

SKILLEN, EDWARD, JR. Review. *Commonweal*, XXXI (March 8, 1940), 438.

NOTES

NOTES

NOTES

NOTES

NOTES

NOTES

NOTES

MONARCH® NOTES AND STUDY GUIDES

ARE AVAILABLE AT RETAIL STORES EVERYWHERE

In the event your local bookseller cannot provide you with other Monarch titles you want —

ORDER ON THE FORM BELOW:

Complete order form appears on inside front & back covers for your convenience.

Simply send retail price, local sales tax, if any, plus 35¢ per book to cover mailing and handling.

TITLE #	AUTHOR & TITLE (exactly as shown on title listing)	PRICE
	PLUS ADDITIONAL 35¢ PER BOOK FOR POSTAGE	
	GRAND TOTAL	$

MONARCH® PRESS, a Simon & Schuster Division of Gulf & Western Corporation
Mail Service Department, 1230 Avenue of the Americas, New York, N.Y. 10020

I enclose $ .... to cover retail price, local sales tax, plus mailing and handling.

Name _____
(Please print)
Address _____
City _____ State _____ Zip _____

Please send check or money order. We cannot be responsible for cash.